T0313669

JoyFull

365 Daily Devotions for Women

Lydia McLaughlin

BroadStreet
PUBLISHING

BroadStreet Publishing® Group, LLC
Savage, Minnesota, USA
BroadStreetPublishing.com

JoyFull: 365 Daily Devotions for Women
Copyright © 2023 Lydia McLaughlin

9781424564736 (faux leather)
9781424564743 (ebook)

Cover and interior by Garborg Design Works | garborgdesign.com

Printed in China

23 24 25 26 27 5 4 3 2 1

This devotional is dedicated to you, sweet sister. I am praying for you. As you seek God through his Word and spend time in it, I am confident that your mind will transform to his will for your life. God is so good and faithful.

Introduction

God often speaks to us through the power of his Word, which is alive and active. It can pierce our souls and speak to our spirits.

I've prayed for Jesus' words to fill the pages of this devotional, and I pray that it leads you closer to him. I pray that it unleashes his power in your heart, ushering you into the throne room of Christ, where we stand in awe at our maker's presence.

I pray that this devotional inspires new habits in us, encouraging us every morning to reach for God's Word first instead of our phones or cups of coffee. Lastly, I pray that our pursuit of his Spirit allows us to experience freedom as we witness his truths become realities. Amen.

January

Alive and Active

The word of God is alive and active. Sharper than any double-edged sword, it penetrates even to dividing soul and spirit, joints and marrow; it judges the thoughts and attitudes of the heart.

HEBREWS 4:12 NIV

Since we are starting a new year together and reading God's Word, I want to begin by acknowledging the power we have at our fingertips when we read the Bible. God's Word is alive and active! Do you believe that?

When we say that God's Word is alive and active, it means that the Bible can speak to us in different ways depending on what we're going through in life. If you are in a time of waiting, then the verses on patience will stick out to you. If you are in a season of uncertainty, God's faithfulness will give you hope. We can be in God's Word during any time of life because it always has fresh, new teachings to inspire us.

Reflect

How much time are you spending in God's Word?
Do you listen to God's voice in your life?

Jesus, I thank you for the power of your Word.
I thank you for meeting me wherever I am
and for always pursuing and loving me. Amen.

The Wilderness

"Forget the former things; do not dwell on the past.
See, I am doing a new thing! Now it springs up;
do you not perceive it? I am making a way in the wilderness
and streams in the wasteland."

ISAIAH 43:18–19 NIV

God is doing a new thing in you. This is his promise.
He declares that he will make streams come forth in the
wastelands. He has made you with your gifts and talents for
such a time as this, and he is making a way for you to use them.

He has a plan for you, and he looks for followers who
will be obedient and bold. Don't give up. Be faithful and
passionate. The hopes and dreams that you carry are inside of
you for a reason. Pursue what you were made for, sweet sister!

Reflect

Look up today's verses in other translations. Consider what
the promises and declarations mean for your life.

Lord, you are faithful. I trust you with my life.
I place my hopes and dreams at your feet.
Lead me according to your will and your way. Amen.

Plans

"For I know the plans I have for you," declares the LORD,
"plans to prosper you and not to harm you,
plans to give you hope and a future."

JEREMIAH 29:11 NIV

In less than a week, God created all that exists, and the Bible is full of prophecies that God fulfilled through Jesus thousands of years later. This is all to say that God knows what he is doing. He promises us in our verse today that he plans for us to prosper and enjoy a future full of hope. He is in control, and we can trust him.

We have the freedom to make plans as well. The anointing on our lives happens when we align our plans with the Lord's. We tend to confine our dreams to boxes of security and comfort. That is, we want God to move as long as the risks to us are minimal. But God's plan falls outside of those neat, comfortable boxes. It's time to step into God's plan!

Reflect

Ask God to reveal the next step of his plan for you.

*Your will, your way, Lord. I desire your plan
for my life over my own. Amen.*

Satisfy My Soul

> "The thief's purpose is to steal and kill and destroy.
> My purpose is to give them a rich and satisfying life."
>
> JOHN 10:10 NLT

Jesus says that he has come to give us a rich and satisfying life. He obviously wasn't saying that he came to fill our homes and garages with a bunch of material things or to busy our calendars with activities. He is saying that he came so that we can have a rich life—a life full of love, joy, and grace. Peace. Adventure.

What satisfies your soul? Dream big and pursue your heart's desires with faith, but also remember that a life like this often won't receive the loudest applause. Jesus offers us a satisfying life, not an easy one.

Reflect

Create a list of things that satisfy your soul.

Lord, thank you for creating me. Thank you for my passions and talents. I submit my life to you, Lord. Amen.

Powerful Spirit

The Spirit of God, who raised Jesus from the dead, lives
in you. And just as God raised Christ Jesus from the dead,
he will give life to your mortal bodies by this same
Spirit living within you.

ROMANS 8:11 NLT

Romans 8:11 is perhaps one of my favorite promises in the
Bible. It promises the most amazing phenomenon: the Spirit
of God lives in you. The same Spirit, the same power that
raised Jesus from the dead, lives in us. Can I get an amen?

If we live out of this truth each day, then our days will
look a lot different. Our minds will be set free, and our joy
will overflow. The ways that we go about our conversations
and tasks will take on new meaning. We must tap into the
Spirit inside of us. That is where we claim a life of freedom.

Reflect

Embrace the power of the Holy Spirit that lives inside of you.

*Jesus, I praise and thank you for your Holy Spirit
living within me. I pray that it will consume me, Lord.
More of you and less of me. Amen.*

Strong Hearts

The eyes of the LORD search the whole earth in order to
strengthen those whose hearts are fully committed to him.

2 CHRONICLES 16:9 NLT

Today's verse is powerful. Imagine God's eyes searching the
world, examining the hearts of his people. Paint it in your
mind: God's eyes running through the scenes of our lives. He
wants his followers to represent him and to be the salt of the
world. I desire for my heart to be fully committed to him so
that he will pour out his strength on to me.

We are all wonderfully made, and each of us is unique.
Maybe you need some of God's strength today. Perhaps you
need purpose or direction. Whatever is going on in your life,
God sees it. His eyes are on your heart, and he is ready to
pour out his strength on to you.

Reflect

Our hearts need to be fully committed to Jesus.
In what areas are you holding back from God?

*Lord, thank you for pouring out your strength onto my life.
You are so good, and I long to serve and be used by you.
It is a deep honor and my heart's desire. Amen.*

Prayer

The heart is deceitful above all things and beyond cure.
Who can understand it?

JEREMIAH 17:9 NIV

We do not have to be taught how to be bad because it is innately within each of us. It's difficult for us to admit our shortcomings or even to recognize the ways that our hearts sometimes steer us in the wrong direction. During prayer time, however, we have a beautiful opportunity to examine ourselves and bring any and all of our shortcomings to the Lord. We can acknowledge our wrongdoings with him and move on.

While you pray, perhaps God will bring to mind a conversation or a friendship that you had not yet realized you handled poorly. Prayer is the perfect time to bring all of your concerns to God.

Reflect

Examine your heart during your prayer time today and ask for forgiveness in any area that needs it.

Lord, I thank you for loving me and always lighting my path. We pray you make me aware of the many ways that I can do better for your glory. Amen.

Blessings

Jabez cried out to the God of Israel, "Oh, that you would bless me and enlarge my territory! Let your hand be with me, and keep me from harm so that I will be free from pain." And God granted his request.

1 CHRONICLES 4:10 NIV

Jabez asks God to bless him in our verse for the day. It's good to ask God for our heart's desires. We want God to bestow upon us the blessings that he designed for us. Jabez asked for God to enlarge his territory, keep him from harm, bless him, and free him from pain.

What are your hopes and dreams? Have you submitted them to Jesus and laid them at God's throne?

Reflect

Spend time with Jesus today. Make your heart's desire known to him and ask him to bless you.

Lord, thank you for my passions, talents, and gifts. You have already blessed me so much with this beautiful life. I pray you would bless me with the desires in my heart. If they are not your will, then I pray you would direct my path for the plan you have for my life. I submit to you, Lord. Amen.

Freedom

The Lord is the Spirit, and where the Spirit of the Lord is,
there is freedom.

2 CORINTHIANS 3:17 NIV

Jesus did not come to simply eliminate our fear of death
but to also give us a life of freedom in this world. We can be
saved by Christ, believe in him, and go to church on Sundays
but still live in bondage. My pastor shared how "secondhand
Christianity" kills people much like secondhand smoke.
Too many of us live off the smoke of someone else's faith,
someone else's fire, or someone else's encounter with Jesus.

Secondhand Christianity cannot and will not satisfy
your faith. God is calling *you*. He has specific plans and a
specific purpose for you according to how he created you.
He came to set you free!

Reflect

Try to identify any chains in your life today. In which areas
have you not submitted to the Lord? Once you identify
them, try handing them over to Jesus.

*Lord, I long to live a life of freedom. I claim the promise of
your Spirit ushering in freedom today. Make that
a reality for me, Lord. Amen.*

Pride

When pride comes, then comes disgrace,
but with humility comes wisdom.

PROVERBS 11:2 NIV

Pride is dangerous. We are to exalt the Lord and consider pride the enemy. We are to pursue humility and see the beauty in its practice. It doesn't take more than a quick scroll on our Instagram feeds to recognize that the biblical value of humility is counter to our culture today. We are conditioned and even encouraged to boast by putting our talents and anything of worldly value on display. This self-pride will create a stronghold and lead to destruction in our lives.

We exist to encounter God and to display his glory. We are to boast in Christ alone, not in our own accomplishments or blessings.

Reflect

Look for opportunities to practice humility today. Acknowledge that your gifts have come from Christ and be mindful of keeping your pride in check.

Lord, I want to be wise. I desire to point people to you and your love. Help me notice the ways in which I am prideful and help me to put my confidence and trust in you. Amen.

Worship

"These people come near to me with their mouth and honor
me with their lips, but their hearts are far from me.
Their worship of me is based on merely human rules
they have been taught."

ISAIAH 29:13 NIV

When my youngest son started kindergarten, the first few
weeks were brutal. He would hold it together all day for his
friends and for his teacher, but the moment he was buckled
into the car, he would have a hardcore meltdown. He would
cry or lose it over small things that ordinarily wouldn't
bother or upset him. I was slow to realize that I should be
thankful for his meltdowns. They meant that he felt safe
enough to lower his guard and experience his big emotions
with me. And you know what? I could handle it. So can God.

God always knows our thoughts, and he isn't impressed
by our ability to hold it all together sometimes. He'd rather
for us to experience our real, honest meltdowns with him
and then draw near to him. That honors him far and above
insincere worship.

Reflect

Have a real, honest conversation with God today.
Ask him questions about things you don't understand.

*Lord, I thank you for wanting a real relationship with me.
Amen.*

Quality Time

Turning around, Jesus saw them following and asked,
"What do you want?"
JOHN 1:38 NIV

Today's verse is the first time that the apostle John, the
author of this Gospel, writes of interacting with Jesus.
Picture yourself looking into the eyes of Jesus before he
poses you a simple yet complex question: "What do you
want?" That question can be answered in so many different
ways, and I think our answers depend on our season of life.
The disciples' answer was simple; they invited Jesus to dine
with them (v. 39). They wanted his company. They wanted to
spend quality time with him.

Everything in our life should be secondary to our
relationship with God. If you are hurting, then spend time
with Jesus. If your marriage is failing, you're stressed about
money, or you're unsatisfied, lonely, or bitter, then spend
time with Jesus. All of those things, as stressful as they are,
can be worked out as we spend time in his presence.

Reflect

Prioritize your time with Jesus today. Imagine yourself
looking into his eyes and telling him what you want.

*Lord, I thank you for caring so much about me. I thank you
for wanting to know my wants and desires. I submit my day to
you, Lord. Reveal yourself to me in new ways. Amen.*

Prepared

We are His work. He has made us to belong to Christ Jesus
so we can work for Him. He planned that we should do this.

EPHESIANS 2:10 NLV

God prepared us and has already given us everything
we need. Think back to a time when you felt completely
prepared for something important. You felt organized, safe,
and secure because you knew you were ready—for the test,
the trip, the event, the meeting, or whatever it was.

When we are prepared, we enjoy a sense of confidence.
We can enjoy that same confidence with our lives because
God created us to do his good works. He has plans for us,
and those plans are our ministry. He has prepared us in this
moment, for this time, with our unique gifts and passions.
You are already prepared and can enjoy confidence because
the Creator of the universe is on your side.

Reflect

Try to shift your mindset today. Imagine God preparing you
for every situation that unfolds throughout your day.

*Thank you, Lord, for creating me and preparing me for this
moment in time and in this place. You are so good, Father.
I love you. Amen.*

Obedience

Loving God means keeping his commandments,
and his commandments are not burdensome.

1 John 5:3 nlt

Many people spend their entire lives searching for their purpose. I spent much of my twenties feeling lost and wondering what to do with my life. I thought I would find a plan and have everything figured out for the rest of my life by the age of twenty-two. I didn't know what I didn't know.

God knows all. He guides us for our best interests. He is trustworthy, so we can trust him. The purpose of our existence is to obey him, love him, and spend time in his presence.

Reflect

Try to obey God in all that you do today. If you feel called by the Holy Spirit to do something, even if it's small, honor that prompting and see what happens.

Lord, I praise you for your guidance. I want to love you well and with my whole heart. Your ways are above mine, and I trust and obey you today. Please help me with my unbelief. Amen.

Dream and Imagine

All glory to God, who is able, through his mighty power
at work within us, to accomplish infinitely more than
we might ask or think.

EPHESIANS 3:20 NLT

There is no limit to what God can do. He's limitless! And he
has given us the ability to dream and imagine because he
wants us to dream and imagine. Our dreams are rooted in
God's power and in what he can do through us, not what we
can do on our own. And because we have the power of God
on our side, it's on us to make our dreams become our reality.

What a gift it is to take bold steps of faith wherever you
feel God calling you. Or if you're unsure, then ask him what
he wants you to do with your life. Reflect in prayer and pay
close attention to anything that excites your spirit.

Reflect

Create a list of ten of your biggest dreams.

*I want to pray big, bold prayers. I want a life full of wonder
and awe. I submit my dreams to you, Lord. Amen.*

Passionate Faith

"No one who puts a hand to the plow and looks back
is fit for service in the kingdom of God."

LUKE 9:62 NIV

In today's verse, Jesus describes a worker who's plowing a field but keeps looking back on his old way of life. In other words, this worker was distracted. But if we are to be passionate about our ministry and about what God is doing today, then we can't spend all of our time and energy looking back on what God called us out of and what he has already done.

Of course, there is a place for remembering God's faithfulness and feeling encouraged by his goodness. Focus on your field, friend! Focus on what God is doing with you right now. Don't be discouraged or distracted by the harvests of others. God has a good crop for you.

Reflect

Consider what God is doing in your life right now. Be a servant who's passionate about your faith.

I thank you for everything that you are doing in my life, Lord. I thank you for my passions and gifts. I pray that I focus on the path on which you are leading me and that I allow only you to fulfill me, Jesus. Amen.

Ambassadors of Heaven

We are therefore Christ's ambassadors, as though God were making his appeal through us. We implore you on Christ's behalf: Be reconciled to God.

2 Corinthians 5:20 niv

An ambassador is often the highest-ranking representative of a territory whose assignment is to represent their homeland in a foreign land. We are Christ's ambassadors, and we represent heaven. What an honor!

Because we serve as ambassadors of Christ, we need to overflow with Christ-centeredness, not self-centeredness, and we need to possess a spirit of excellence. Today's culture lacks excellence and, instead, favors efficiency. But if we do everything to our greatest ability while representing our maker, the world around us will take notice. We change the course of our lives when we know who we are and what we are created to do, so let's represent excellence to the world around us.

Reflect

Select an inspiring Bible verse that captures who you truly are in Christ. Memorize this promise and remind yourself of it today and throughout the week.

Lord, thank you for choosing me to represent you. Thank you for loving me like a precious daughter. It is the honor of my life to be seen, known, and loved by you. Amen.

Hope of Glory

*To them God has chosen to make known among
the Gentiles the glorious riches of this mystery,
which is Christ in you, the hope of glory.*

COLOSSIANS 1:27 NIV

This "hope of glory" mentioned in Colossians is our faith, our "glorious riches." We don't need to have every detail of our faith figured out, but God does call us to have it. And we can grow and cultivate our faith by spending time in God's Word. His presence will bring us contentment and remind us of just how much we have to be thankful for, and a grateful heart often means a content soul.

When you focus on our Creator, the issues of this world tend to fade away. Because no matter what season of life you find yourself in, you are never outside God's love, provision, promises, or goodness.

Reflect

Sit with the concept of the "hope of glory" living within you. What does that phrase mean to you personally?

*Thank you, Lord, for living in me. I am grateful for
the mystery of our faith and the hope that you give us
in Christ's glory. Amen.*

Christ in Us

"I have been crucified with Christ and I no longer live, but Christ lives in me. The life I now live in the body, I live by faith in the Son of God, who loved me and gave himself for me."

GALATIANS 2:20 NIV

Although we are literally alive, our concept of self died when we welcomed Jesus into our hearts. In the waiting, in the hopelessness, in the good times and the bad, "I no longer live."

Our ego is difficult to dethrone, and that pesky sense of self will always try to crawl its way back to its former throne. But we made the powerful, life-giving choice to submit to our maker, and this verse promises us that Christ now lives where our self once lived.

Reflect

Approach your day from the perspective that you no longer live but that Jesus lives in you. In every word you speak and in every action you take.

Lord, I want to live my life boldly by faith in you, Jesus. Thank you for your love. Thank you for your goodness and grace. I pray to be a light to the people you put in my path today. Amen.

Peace

Let us aim for harmony in the church
and try to build each other up.

ROMANS 14:19 NLT

Boundaries bring peace to our life. I personally believe that setting boundaries is biblical. God set boundaries with us, and we refer to them as his Commandments. He put them in place for our own good, and in the same way, boundaries are blessings not only to ourselves but also to the people we share relationships with. They protect us and help us live peacefully with the world around us.

Today's verse also calls us to build each other up. That means our words should be edifying, compassionate, and spoken out of love over one another. It's easier said than done, at times, but remember that we are called to a higher standard.

Reflect

Be intentional about building up someone in your life today.

I pray for a peaceful life. I want to be someone who isn't easily offended but full of peace. Fill me with your presence, Lord, and let me speak with the love and hope that only your Spirit can bring. Amen.

Just the Right Time

Let's not get tired of doing what is good. At just the right time we will reap a harvest of blessing if we don't give up.

GALATIANS 6:9 NLT

I love the first five words in the second part of today's verse: "At just the right time." Those words are so important for us to always remember. In the Bible, God waited to send his son, Jesus Christ, until the perfect time. We serve a patient God who is the Creator of everything and the King of time.

So trust the timing of your life. Trust that God knows what he is doing and that his timing is perfect. He's got you. Do not tire of doing good because God will show up at just the right time.

Reflect

Repeat to yourself throughout the day, "At just the right time." Remind yourself as many times as you need to that God is on your side and that you can trust his timing.

Lord, I want to do what is good and pleasing in your sight. I want to be available to serve you. I want to trust you with every aspect of my life, including your timing. I trust you, Lord. Amen.

Heavenly Perspective

Make it your goal to live a quiet life, minding your own business and working with your hands, just as we instructed you before. Then people who are not believers will respect the way you live, and you will not need to depend on others.

1 Thessalonians 4:11–12 NLT

We are called to mind our own business. This doesn't mean we have to turn a blind eye to injustice, but it does mean that we need to have an eternal perspective. When we are busy looking up toward heaven, the nonsense around us won't distract or offend us.

If we want to do well, we have to be well. Whatever is going on inside of us will also flow out of us. So if we want our thoughts to overflow with love and gratitude, then we need our spirits to be consumed with Jesus.

Reflect

Monitor your thoughts carefully today. Listen to the words that leave your mouth. Are you orienting yourself and the people around you toward heaven?

I invite your Holy Spirit into my heart, my mind, and my words, Lord. I desire to overflow with your love and kindness. Amen.

Godly Life

His divine power has given us everything we need for a
godly life through our knowledge of him who called us
by his own glory and goodness.

2 PETER 1:3 NIV

God has given us everything we need to lead godly lives. Let
yourself steep in that truth. Let it sink deeply into your heart
and mind. When we know that God has given us all that
we need for every situation and circumstance, our outlook,
actions, and thoughts change. We become more confident,
secure, and rooted in our faith.

How do we live a godly life? Today's verse holds the key:
"through our knowledge of him." We gain this knowledge by
spending time in his Word, in prayer, and in his presence. It
also helps to invest in a faith-filled community of friends and
mentors who know us well and point us to Jesus.

Reflect

Come up with one way to pursue God on a deeper level
today, whether that's meditating on today's verse, proudly
sharing it with another person, or connecting with Jesus
in your own way.

*Father, I praise you for your goodness and glory! Thank you
for being so beautiful and kind. Thank you for your beauty all
over this earth. I pray that I can know you deeper today and
make you proud. Amen.*

Stand Firm

Stand firm…with the belt of truth buckled around your waist, with the breastplate of righteousness in place, and with your feet fitted with the readiness that comes from the gospel of peace…Take up the shield of faith, with which you can extinguish all the flaming arrows of the evil one.
Take the helmet of salvation and the sword of the Spirit, which is the word of God.

EPHESIANS 6:14–17 NIV

These verses are so rich with inspiration that it's no wonder why they're so popular. The Lord's power gives us strength. Do you feel in step with God's mighty power? Make space in your life for him to display it. Create rhythms in your life that allow God to speak to you through his Word. Worship him in the car during your commute or spend time in prayer inviting him into your daily routine.

Once we allow ourselves to live boldly for Christ, our lives transform. God wants to use our stories for his glory.

Reflect

Stand firm, sweet sister! Be ready for spiritual battle daily and be prepared to win.

I pray that you continue to open up my spirit so that I can understand and live in all of the powerful promises that you gave me through your Word, Lord.

Growing Pains

> No discipline seems pleasant at the time, but painful.
> Later on, however, it produces a harvest of righteousness
> and peace for those who have been trained by it.
>
> HEBREWS 12:11 NIV

We will experience pain and discomfort in this life. It is not necessarily to discourage us from our purpose or spiritual pursuits. Just like I lovingly discipline my kids so that they can grow into healthy adults, God can and often does use our discomfort and pain for good. For example, when someone hurts us, our painful experience sometimes shows us that our relationship with that person might not be a healthy one. And sometimes our pain draws us closer to God.

We are stronger than we think. We must hand over our pain to God and trust that he is doing good things in and for us. Always.

Reflect

When something inevitably goes awry or doesn't go your way today, shift your mindset. Ask yourself what quality God may be harvesting in you, such as patience, forgiveness, gentleness, or another positive quality.

Thank you for caring for me, Lord. At times, you teach me in ways I do not understand, but I trust you, Jesus, and praise you for all you are doing with me and my life. Amen.

Bloom Where You're Planted

The righteous choose their friends carefully,
but the way of the wicked leads them astray.

PROVERBS 12:26 NIV

It's important to make wise choices about the people we choose to surround ourselves with. And there's wisdom in pursuing and nurturing the friendships that God puts in our lives. My best friend from childhood, who lovingly served as maid of honor at my wedding, doesn't live in the same state as I do. Our kids don't go to the same school. I don't get to do life with her like I want to, and our friendship doesn't look the same as it did when we lived in the same town, but it doesn't mean that I love her any less.

Relationships and friendships change. Not only is that normal, but it's also healthy. Consider the people you see on a regular basis. Pursue and invest in the healthy, godly relationships. Bloom where you are planted.

Reflect

Examine the friends that God has placed in your life. Invest in at least one of these friendships today, whether that's sending a quick text to tell them something kind, scheduling a lunch, or saying a prayer for them.

Lord, I thank you for my friendships. Help me be a good
friend so my life can be full. I place my heart at your feet,
Lord. Lead me today and always. Amen.

Precious as Gold

He knows the way that I take;
when he has tested me,
I will come forth as gold.

JOB 23:10 NIV

Sometimes God tests us, and sometimes his will for us is to walk through fire. Remember that he's after our hearts, and by walking through fire, he allows our hearts to become refined. When we emerge on the other side, we become more precious than gold.

Some of us might feel as though God is testing us in life, and I encourage you, precious friend, to walk through that fire with hope and faith in Jesus. Just as Job declares, so do we, "I will come forth as gold." Let the Lord test you, and have the confidence today to know that you will come forth more precious and valuable than gold.

Reflect

Make Job's prayer yours: "Lord, I will come forth as gold."

I pray for all the ways in which I am being tried and tested right now. I want all that remains in me to shine like gold and point people to you, Jesus. Amen.

Suffering

"I have indeed seen the misery of my people in Egypt.
I have heard them crying out because of their slave drivers,
and I am concerned about their suffering."

EXODUS 3:7 NIV

In the very next verse in Exodus, God declares that he's going to rescue his people from the Egyptians and bring them to "a land flowing with milk and honey" (v. 8). We can find comfort in these two verses because they show us just how much he loves us.

God sees you. Like he did with the Israelites, God hears your cries and is concerned for you. This does not mean that he will make all things perfect and magical, like a fairy godmother. After all, he led his people in the desert for forty years before they entered the promised land. But he gives you the power of his Holy Spirit. He cracks open your hurt and walks with you in times of challenge.

Reflect

Think of a time in your life when you felt God's presence
while experiencing pain—physical or emotional.
Thank him for that season and his comforting presence
during your prayer time today.

*Lord, you are Creator of this world, and I trust you.
I don't understand your ways, but still I worship you,
for I know that you are good. Amen.*

Wonderfully Made

I praise you because I am fearfully and wonderfully made.
PSALM 139:14 NIV

Comparison is a trap, and it steals our joy. It causes us so much pain when we try to be people we aren't. God designed us with gifts specific and unique to each and every one of us. Only we can accomplish the things that God has set for us to do.

Fix your eyes on what lies before you and you alone. Focus on your own life, worries, blessings, and gifts. Stay in your lane. Whatever God has desired and planned for you is already yours. Another you will never exist, and you are wonderfully made, sweet friend. Own it!

Reflect

Stop comparing yourself to others. Be mindful of your thinking patterns today and steer your thoughts clear of the trap of comparison.

Thank you for making me so wonderfully, Lord. You have given me beautiful talents and gifts, and it is my heart's desire to honor you with the blessings that you have given me. I praise you, Jesus. Amen.

Life Reflects the Heart

As water reflects the face,
so one's life reflects the heart.

PROVERBS 27:19 NIV

I love the wisdom in Proverbs. It can be such a simple truth, but it holds so much weight if we pause and apply it to our lives. If someone were to look at your life today, what would they see? What are you investing your time in? Whom are you investing your time in? What does your life truly reflect? Is your schedule today filled with appointments to further God's kingdom or your own?

Of course, we should pursue our passion and ambitions, but do they glorify Jesus? I have heard it said that you can tell where your heart is by looking at your bank account. Time and money are of great value to us. How are you spending yours?

Reflect

Take a personal inventory of how
you spend your money and time today.

Lord, my heart is pursuing you. I pray my life will always reflect that. You are my King, and I surrender to you, Lord. Amen.

To the Full

> "I have come that they may have life,
> and have it to the full."
>
> JOHN 10:10 NIV

I love to host parties and entertain. It's not stressful for me to host large numbers of people in my home. Dinner for forty on Saturday? Sounds fun. Can't wait! Volunteer in the children's ministry on Sunday? That's my nightmare. It stresses me out and brings me no joy, and I'm sure the little kiddos would agree. God didn't give me that gift, and that's okay. He gave me so many other gifts that allow me to serve him with gladness.

Jesus wants us to live a life full of freedom and joy. He wants us to enjoy one another. That's why he came to earth. God wants us to be content in our gifts and in ourselves, as the people he created us to be. Do you feel you're living your life to the fullest?

Reflect

Think about your gifts. How can you intentionally use
your gifts today to serve someone else?

Lord, I pray for a full life. I want to be someone who overflows with joy and contentment. I thank you for making me whole and loving me so well. I offer you my praise, Jesus. Amen.

February

Beautiful Words

Never let ugly or hateful words come from your mouth, but instead let your words become beautiful gifts that encourage others; do this by speaking words of grace to help them.

EPHESIANS 4:29 TPT

I love The Passion Translation for Scripture like today's. The words paint a powerful picture in my mind. I want my words to be beautiful gifts of encouragement to those around me. I don't want them to be ugly and hateful.

Have you ever been around someone who only seems to talk about other people? What about someone who is super negative? We get to choose the people we invite into our homes, hearts, and lives, and we can choose to be beacons of light to those around us by speaking words of grace. Guard yourself and be wise.

Reflect

Try to speak only beautiful and uplifting words today. Think about what comes out of your mouth and try to uplift and encourage everyone God puts in your path.

I thank you for your love and mercy, Lord. I want to speak goodness and love over everyone you place in my path today. Let me offer to them encouraging, life-giving words. Amen.

New Creation

Anyone who belongs to Christ has become a new person.
The old life is gone; a new life has begun!

2 Corinthians 5:17 NLT

When the devil tries to haunt us with our past, we can find ourselves stuck in an unhealthy cycle of remembering and reliving the pains and shame of yesterday. In times like this, we need to boldly proclaim the promise that Christ tells us of our future.

Jesus didn't come down to earth and conquer death just to get you into heaven. He came to set us free. He makes us new, and his kingdom of heaven lives inside each of us.

Reflect

Whenever you find yourself dwelling on your current problems or past mistakes, offer up a prayer of gratitude and thanksgiving. Take note of how this simple act changes your mindset today.

*Jesus, I praise you for making me a new creation.
I am covered in your love and grace, and I bow down at
your feet. I give you my past, my present, and my future.
You are King of my life, and I worship you. Amen.*

Bless My Enemies

"I tell you, love your enemies
and pray for those who persecute you."
MATTHEW 5:44 NIV

When we pray for our enemies, we are consciously choosing to submit to God's plan and to lay our pain and pride at his throne. Although our enemies wrong us, we choose to lift them up and pray for their blessings. This practice may not come easily or naturally, but praying for our enemies fosters deep spiritual healing.

We want to believe that once we forgive someone, that's that. But rarely is that ever the case because forgiveness is a process. We need to forgive as many times as we are hurt, so whenever feelings of anger or hurt bubble up inside us, we need to submit those feelings to the Lord and choose forgiveness. He is the one who will remove the hurt. Remember that our power lies in our ability to forgive those who hurt us.

Reflect

Say a prayer for someone who has hurt you.

I believe in the power of prayer, Lord. I believe in your healing hand. I pray that I won't hold on to bitterness. Instead, I pray for those who have hurt me. Bless them today. Amen.

Spiritual Battle

Our struggle is not against flesh and blood, but against the rulers, against the authorities, against the powers of this dark world and against the spiritual forces of evil in the heavenly realms.

EPHESIANS 6:12 NIV

We are at war—make no mistake about it, friend. I want to focus on our social media use today. I hear so many women talk about mindlessly scrolling on social media, but it is not mindless. All of those images, opinions, videos, and messages affect us. Some are encouraging, entertaining, and educational, but some are harmful.

Guard your social media feeds by choosing content that uplifts you and adds positivity to your life instead of stealing your joy, peace, and confidence. Hold yourself accountable for how much time you are spending on your phone versus how much time you are spending in God's Word. We should fill our minds with God's truth more than anything else.

Reflect

Set a boundary with your social media use, whether it's setting a time limit or unfollowing users whose content makes you feel bad about yourself and others.

Thank you for being a mighty God. You are all-powerful, and all of creation bows at your feet. I thank you for being my King, my God, and my Savior. Amen.

Truth and Wisdom

You want truth deep within the heart.
And You will make me know wisdom in the hidden part.

PSALM 51:6 NLV

Jesus didn't just bleed on the cross; he also bruised, which is the result of an injury to internal blood vessels. When we think about his suffering symbolically, he bled on the outside of his body in sacrifice for our actions, and he bled on the inside to represent forgiveness of our thoughts. This shows us that God cares about our thoughts and our deeds because he's concerned for our souls. He's always pursuing our true love and admiration. He wants our true selves and our honest worship.

The second part of this promise is equally beautiful and powerful. If we feel lost, then all we need to do is call on God, and he will give us wisdom. The devil is the author of confusion, but our God is clear. Wisdom is found in the Lord.

Reflect

We want to be wise in our words, actions, and decisions.
Ask God for wisdom today.

*Lord, thank you for your wisdom. Thank you for revealing
yourself to me every day and for giving me clarity
to direct my path today. Amen.*

Gentleness

As God's chosen people, holy and dearly loved, clothe
yourselves with compassion, kindness, humility,
gentleness and patience.

COLOSSIANS 3:12 NIV

Each of the qualities in today's verse offers so much richness,
but let's focus on gentleness today. The Greek word for
gentleness is *praotes*, which is a "meekness."[1] I picture
gentleness not as an outward feeling but as a calmness,
particularly toward God.

Gentleness is possessing the faith, trust, and strength
to submit to God's will, and it pours out of us when our
souls are calmed by the trust we have in our maker. I
personally feel like I've fought with God many times before
remembering that he is trustworthy, which always restores
my calmness. Our God *is* trustworthy, and we are his chosen
daughters.

Reflect

How might you be wrestling with God? Which area of your
life do you need to surrender to him?

*I want to be a source of kindness and humility to those around
me. Fill my heart with your Holy Spirit, Lord, and let me
overflow with the fruits of being in your presence. Amen.*

---

1   James Strong, *Strong's Expanded Exhaustive Concordance of
the Bible* (Nashville: Thomas Nelson, 2009), #4236.

Healthy Friendship

Rejoice with those who rejoice,
weep with those who weep.

ROMANS 12:15 ESV

The adventure of life is not meant to be lived alone. God has made us to share life experiences with one another. Even Jesus sent his disciples out two by two. But comparison, jealousy, and envy have no place in a healthy friendship.

Godly sisters in Christ cheer each other on and share in each other's sorrows. When our friends have success, we celebrate them as their greatest cheerleaders. When they hurt, we hurt, and their tears become our tears. When we are healthy mentally and spiritually, we can form wonderful friendships, which are a beautiful gift from God.

Reflect

I challenge you to invest your time in a Bible study group with women who attend your church or live near you. If you are already in a Bible study group, then I challenge you to tell a friend how special she is to you. Try to tell her face-to-face, but if that's not possible, a phone call or text is good too.

Thank you for the people you've placed in my life, Lord. I want to be a good friend. I pray for the friends who come to my mind right now and ask that you bless them today. Amen.

Transformation

Do not conform to the pattern of this world, but be transformed by the renewing of your mind. Then you will be able to test and approve what God's will is—his good, pleasing and perfect will.

ROMANS 12:2 NIV

It's easy to settle on a world view that isn't godly, but God's view is that of heaven. There's no anger or gossip in heaven, so we shouldn't settle for that in our lives on earth either. We can't lead a life full of light and joy like we're supposed to if our minds are preoccupied with dark, worldly thoughts.

We have the choice to either conform to the world or transform the world, but if we want to transform the world, then we have to be intentional about shifting our mindsets and placing our identities in Jesus. Today, let's begin to attest to God's pleasing and perfect will.

Reflect

Identify an area in your life in which you have allowed the world to dictate your expectations. Make a promise to yourself to shift your thinking to enjoy a renewed, godly mindset.

Lord, I believe your will is good and pleasing.
Transform my thoughts to be your thoughts, Jesus.
I want more of you. Amen.

Gratitude

Give thanks in all circumstances;
for this is God's will for you in Christ Jesus.

1 Thessalonians 5:18 niv

We all strive for gratitude, and maybe that's why #grateful has over fifty million tags on Instagram. As I scrolled through the posts with that hashtag, most of the images were of happy moments and smiles. It wasn't necessarily surprising, but we are called to give thanks in all circumstances, not just the happy ones. We should give thanks in times of trial, heartbreak, and turmoil too.

A truly grateful heart comes from a content soul. And a content soul comes from taking the focus off ourselves and our circumstances and realizing how good our maker is. When we appreciate God and his love for us, we can't help but fall to our knees in thanks.

Reflect

Spend time thinking about all of the work that God has done in your life and thank him for it today.

I praise you for who you are, Lord. I praise you for your goodness and faithfulness, and I am so grateful for the day ahead of me. I know it holds the good plans that you have for me. Amen.

Love at All Times

A friend loves at all times.

PROVERBS 17:17 NIV

Proverbs is a book of wisdom found in the Bible, and so many of its verses stress the importance of guarding our tongue. This piece of wisdom holds so very true in friendships. Our words are powerful and can be used as weapons, especially against those closest to us. That's why we are not to gossip or break our friends' confidence.

In order to have a friendship that stands the test of time, we must cover our friends in love like Jesus did. He perfectly exemplified the qualities of a good friend. He loved at all times, he forgave, and he was loyal. He understood patience and grace. We'll mess up and make mistakes from time to time, but even when we do, we can still choose to love and honor our friends by asking forgiveness, taking responsibility, and making amends.

Reflect

Pray for your friendships today. If one of them is struggling or experiencing tension, reach out to that friend to resolve whatever conflict you might be experiencing. Make amends and cover her in love.

Lord, thank you for the women you have placed in my life to be my soul sisters. Help me to see new ways for me to encourage and love them well. Amen.

Rejoice

Instead of your shame you will receive a double portion,
and instead of disgrace you will rejoice in your inheritance.
And so you will inherit a double portion in your land, and
everlasting joy will be yours.

ISAIAH 61:7 NIV

In today's verse, the Lord promises not only to make things right but also to repay us double. Only God can work like that. And we can expect him to use whatever has caused us pain or shame for his glory. Shame is never from the Lord. The Holy Spirit convicts us of our actions, but shame is neither from God nor does it serve us.

That's why we walk toward Jesus. When we walk with him, our soul sparkles. Our face shines bright, and we become a new creation. We don't have to let our past define or control us, and we never have to relive whatever pain and guilt might haunt us. Today is a new day, sister. Let's end that damaging cycle once and for all.

Reflect

When you begin to think back on a past experience or decision that made you feel shame, don't hold on to it any longer. Release that to Jesus today.

Thank you, Jesus, for replacing my shame with your everlasting joy. You make my heart soar with your promises. I believe them and claim them over my life. Amen.

True Beauty

Those who look to him are radiant;
their faces are never covered with shame.
PSALM 34:5 NIV

Society values and praises physical beauty. It's human nature to want to feel praised, yet God values that which is found within. As his Son told us, we are to serve, be generous, and give with open hands. That's true beauty.

God's standard turns our natural desire for praise on its head, so how can that satisfy us and lead us to joy? Well, an old adage comes to my mind: whatever you feed will grow. That is, if you try being a servant even when you don't want to, then you will cultivate within yourself the heart of a servant. And if you are kingdom-focused, then your mind, too, will transform and be filled with beautiful, godly thoughts.

Reflect

Who in your life is beautiful and radiant because of her faith? Share that thought with her today.

Lord, I come before you with an open heart and a desire to glorify you in all my words, all my deeds, and all my thoughts. I want to radiate with your glory shining through me. Thank you for your Word and for your love. Amen.

Kingdom Focused

Set your minds on things above,
not on earthly things.

COLOSSIANS 3:2 NIV

Through the Holy Spirit, Paul tells us in today's verse to
"set [our] minds." Now focus on that phrase. It's an internal
action that we can pursue and practice, but it requires
us to make an effort. We aren't magically freed from the
temptations and darkness of this world simply because we go
to church or attend a Bible study or because we call ourselves
believers. We must make a conscious, purposeful, faithful
effort if we want to have faithful actions. It's how we die to
ourselves so that we can live for Christ.

We set our mind on things above by fixing our eyes
on the path that God has set us on and placing our trust in
Jesus. We also need to watch and guard our thoughts. That
means we must be mindful of our Instagram scrolling and
the conversations we have on the daily. We must also watch
where we allow our minds to wander.

Reflect

What changes can you make to your daily life
to help you set your mind on things above?

*Today I set my mind on things that concern you, Lord.
Let my thoughts be kingdom-focused and help me see
through your eyes. Fill my spirit with yours. Amen.*

Tough Conversations

A brother is born to help in time of need.
PROVERBS 17:17 NLT

Have you ever walked through hardship with a friend but continue to watch her make one bad decision after another? Can I get an amen that trying to correct some friends, even gently and lovingly, is like walking into a fire? Friendships need to be rooted in honesty; otherwise, what is the point?

Yet we know that if we enter difficult conversations from a place of love, we will leave that conversation with a friendship built on solid rock. We all want healthy, real, safe friendships. They require work and sometimes disagreements and fights. As Proverbs reassures us, a brother (or sister!) is made for hard times and times of need. Remember that relationships bound by the Holy Spirit will withstand tests of adversity.

Reflect

Consider your friendships. Are you speaking honesty over them or tickling their ears with lies? If you've been procrastinating a tough conversation, then make a plan to set out and have it. Remember to come from a place of love.

Lord, thank you for the women and friendships you have placed in my life. I pray for the hard times that my loved ones might be facing, and I ask you to make me a source of strength for them. Amen.

Perfect Timing

When the set time had fully come,
God sent his Son.

GALATIANS 4:4 NIV

The entire Bible begins with the phrase "In the beginning." This may give us pause since we know that the Trinity is beyond space and time, and yet the Bible references the concept of time in the very first sentence. Perhaps we can assume that time was the first thing God created.

God is patient, my friend. He created the whole world and then waited patiently to send his Son to redeem us. He can take our fire, our desert, our pain, and our circumstances and turn them into glory for him. That is the business that God is in. He created time and understands the importance of waiting for the *right* time. Find comfort in knowing that he is for us and that he, too, knows what it feels like to wait. Find joy in knowing that we will come forth as gold.

Reflect

**Submit your worries to Jesus and trust God
with the timing of your life.**

*You created everything, including time, Lord.
I trust your timing for my life. Amen.*

Spirit within Us

"The Kingdom of God is within you."

LUKE 17:21 TLB

We weren't made to allow gossip, addiction, depression, anger, and other negativity to rule us, but many of us find ourselves unhappy in certain areas of life because we've allowed the world's point of view to placate us. We end up focusing on things that do not determine our value: the clothes we wear, the car we drive, and the weight of our bodies. But we were not made to have space in our lives and minds for such trivial things. We could spend our whole lives working an awful job or chasing money, power, or security, but the true cost of those pursuits is our joy.

Instead, we need to be kingdom-focused. Jesus says that the kingdom of God is inside us, so, of course, we feel off or dissatisfied when God's spirit is extinguished. But because his Spirit lives within us, we can lead lives full of his heavenly kingdom. When we focus on the Lord and things above, the elements of this world truly fall away, and our faces shine brightly, full of beauty.

Reflect

Focus today on living out the kingdom of God through your thoughts, words, and actions.

Lord, I praise you for your kingdom, your plan, and your ways. I submit all to you, Jesus. Amen.

Encouragement

Teach a child to choose the right path,
and when he is older, he will remain upon it.
PROVERBS 22:6 TLB

It's our job as parents to know our children's gifts and passions, help them pursue them, and build them up in those areas. The same is true for us personally. That is, we are to know our own passions and talents and to be content with the gifts that God has given us.

This truth can also be applied to friendships. I speak to some friends on the phone every day, and others I only text on occasion. I love and consider all of them to be close friends. But every friendship is different. Our bonds are different. Perhaps you feel hurt by one friend who's super close with another. As difficult as it sounds, don't leave room for envy or comparison. Remember comparison is the thief of joy. Instead be thankful for the friends the Lord has put in your life.

Reflect

Think about the gifts your kids have. How can you encourage them? If you don't have kids, think of your closest friends who could use some encouragement today.

*Thank you for creating everyone so differently, Lord.
I want to see the gifts and talents of the people around me so that I may encourage them and glorify you. Amen.*

Talents and Passions

God has given each of you some special abilities; be sure to use them to help each other, passing on to others God's many kinds of blessings. Are you called to preach? Then preach as though God himself were speaking through you. Are you called to help others? Do it with all the strength and energy that God supplies so that God will be glorified through Jesus Christ—to him be glory and power forever and ever.

1 PETER 4:10–11 TLB

I know today's passage is long, but it's worth it. These verses remind us that it's silly and small of us to compare our blessings with someone else's because, at the end of the day, our gifts were given to us through the grace of God and for his glory. Read that again: our gifts are to glorify God.

When we compare ourselves to others, we aren't celebrating or resting in the reality that God created us, cherishes us, and loves us. And he knows the desires of our heart, so let's fix our eyes on the path God has set before us today and see things with an eternal mindset. That is where God's glory shines, and nothing compares to that.

Reflect

Identify five of your talents and passions.
How can you use them to glorify God?

Lord, thank you for my talents and blessings. Amen.

Praise Him

I will exalt you, my God the King; I will praise your name
for ever and ever. Every day I will praise you and extol your
name for ever and ever. Great is the LORD and most worthy
of praise; his greatness no one can fathom.

PSALMS 145:1–3 NIV

Praise is the response of a grateful heart, and it honors God.
It is his will for us to praise him in all circumstances, as it
ushers us into his presence, where we fall more and more in
love with his Spirit.

Have you trained your heart to praise him regardless of
circumstances, in good times and bad? When things don't
go your way, are you the first to complain, or do you choose
to have a thankful posture? Remember that God is always
good, and we praise him because of who he is. His goodness
doesn't change because of our circumstances, so neither
should our posture of praise.

Reflect

Take time today to praise God for who he is and all that he's
doing. Praise his name freely.

*I praise you, Lord! You are mighty and good. You forgive, and
you love. I praise you for your creation and for who you are.
Thank you for creating me. Amen.*

You Harvest What You Plant

> You will always harvest what you plant.
> GALATIANS 6:7 NLT

We've all heard the old adage "we reap what we sow." Therefore, we need to set boundaries to protect ourselves from the pitfalls of this world and the harm it can do to us spiritually, mentally, and emotionally. Yes, grace and forgiveness are found in Jesus, and he can heal us, but our actions always have consequences, sometimes positive and sometimes negative.

Take social media for example. Personally, I can be in a great mood, even the best mood, but then I hop on Instagram to find that all of my friends hung out and failed to invite me. Next thing I know, I'm feeling down and rejected. It's moments like these when we need to protect our minds. We live today through the thoughts and actions of our past, so let's be intentional with our efforts in planting good seeds of the Spirit.

Reflect

Examine your actions over the past week. What good seeds did you plant? Ask God for forgiveness for any bad seeds you might have planted.

I desire a full life and a plentiful harvest, Lord.
Thank you for your grace as I press on toward
all you have planned for me. Amen.

He Takes Care of Us

They confidently trust the LORD to care for them.

PSALM 112:7 NLT

To do something confidently means that you have little or no doubt about your abilities or the outcome of what you are undertaking. Do you believe that God has the ability to take care of you, or do you doubt or feel skeptical of that promise?

Rest assured that we have the gift of confidence in God. That is, we can confidently pray and ask him to take care of us—because what matters to us matters to God. Let's be women who confidently trust that God will take care of us today.

Reflect

Pray with confidence today. Be specific about
what you need for God to take care of for you.

*Lord, I pray that you will take care of my needs today.
My desires, my worries, and my dreams. I submit all
of myself to you. Take care of me. You are my good,
good Father, and I trust you, Jesus. Amen.*

A Servant's Heart

"Who is greater, the one who is at the table or the one who serves?…I am among you as one who serves."

LUKE 22:27 NIV

We want people to admire us, but Jesus tells us to serve. We want what we believe is ours because we think we deserve it, but Jesus tells us to be generous and to give with open hands. We revere physical beauty, but God sees beauty within. God's way is the opposite of the world, and that's a beautiful truth.

How does turning our natural desires on their heads satisfy us and lead us to joy? Think of our devotion from two days ago: we reap what we sow. If we are intentional about serving, especially when we don't necessarily want to, then we cultivate a servant's heart within ourselves. When we are kingdom-focused, our hearts and minds transform.

Reflect

Ask yourself how you can serve Jesus today
and put it into action.

Lord, thank you for the beautiful example of servitude that you have given me. You loved people so well, and I pray that your Holy Spirit will guide me to love people well today and every day. Amen.

Life-Giving Promises

Godliness with contentment is great gain.

1 Timothy 6:6 niv

True contentment comes when we are focused on and bound to Christ. That's why we need to seek God and know his promises. We need to shift our focus from ourselves and from pleasing others and instead actively pursue our faith in God. When we do this, we can lead a life of freedom, just as Jesus calls us to do.

But how can we expect to know how to lead a life of freedom? By remembering that abundant life is not based on our circumstances or our mood but in our knowledge of Jesus' promises. By having a solid grasp on God's Word, we can feel secure not only in our belief in him but also in his life-giving promises.

Reflect

Make your prayer life the highlight of your day,
not just another item on your to-do list,
by memorizing one of God's promises today.

I want to pursue you today, Jesus. Help me let go of my ego and my tendency to focus on myself and help me shift my focus on you. You are all I need. Amen.

The Power of Love

"My command is this:
Love each other as I have loved you."
JOHN 15:12 NIV

We are called to love others, yet society has given us permission to mess this up. Cancel culture has allowed us to forget what it looks like to love others because we have forgotten or misunderstood just how much God loves us. We are his chosen people, and he not only tells but also shows us over and over in the Bible how dearly beloved we are. He declares that he is for us and continually makes plans to rescue us, no matter how many times we forsake him.

Because we can't overflow what isn't inside of us, our first step in loving those around us is to allow ourselves to be loved by God. We are daughters of the King! We have authority and power in him. We are chosen and created to be the power of the Holy Spirit in this world right now, and we can show that power through love.

Reflect

Embrace God's love for you today, whether through rest, prayer, words, actions, or another meaningful way. What does this kind of embracing look like for you?

Thank you for loving me, Lord. I pray that I will be your vessel to love others well. Amen.

Guilt versus Shame

"When the Helper comes, He will show the world the truth about sin. He will show the world about being right with God. And He will show the world what it is to be guilty."

JOHN 16:8 NLV

This verse contains the words of Jesus as he describes the Holy Spirit to his apostles. When it comes to the Holy Spirit, we know that it lives inside of us. It sometimes convicts us, too, so I want to touch on the difference between shame and guilt.

The Holy Spirit convicts us, which is when we feel guilty for our actions, words, or thoughts. But once we confess our sins and ask for forgiveness, God forgets them, and we are fully forgiven. Whereas guilt says, "I feel bad," shame says, "I am bad." Shame does not come from the Lord, friend. It serves no one but the devil, and it's a twisted emotion. To live in it is a trap set by the enemy. Any time we begin to feel shame, we must remember to place our trust in the Lord, who loves us endlessly.

Reflect

Spend time specifically communing with the Holy Spirit today. Think of a time when you felt shame and then proclaim your worth in God.

Lord, I thank you for the Holy Spirit. I want to know you more, on a deeper level, and in new ways. I am yours, God. Amen.

Bless Me, Lord

Jabez cried out to the God of Israel, "Oh, that you would bless me and enlarge my territory! Let your hand be with me, and keep me from harm so that I will be free from pain." And God granted his request.

1 CHRONICLES 4:10 NIV

God wants our hearts to align with his will so that he can give us the desires of our heart, just as he did for Jabez, who boldly asked God to bless him. Are you afraid to ask God to bless you?

It is important that we spend time with Jesus every day to consciously align ourselves with his Holy Spirit and commune with his presence. When we do that, our hearts align with his, and the desires of our hearts transform to want the things that he created us for. And whatever God wants for us is always best. Start making room for whatever you're praying for because it's on its way.

Reflect

During your prayer time today, ask God to bless you with his favor and anoint you. Tell him what that looks like to you and open yourself up to what it could look like in God's plan for your life.

Bless me, Father. Be with me in all that I do and everything that I pursue. I ask for your favor, Lord. Direct my path so that my heart aligns with your will. Amen.

Set Free

It is for freedom that Christ has set us free.
Stand firm, then, and do not let yourselves
be burdened again by a yoke of slavery.

GALATIANS 5:1 NIV

We can be held captive by many things, but the most common things that I see holding people back today are doubt, loneliness, insecurity, anger, anxiety, fear, materialism, and depression. I'm sure we could add more (and then more) to the list, but no matter what might hold us captive, Christ can set us free. He came to restore the broken.

When we live a life seeking the Spirit of the Lord, he enters into the spaces where we invite him and sets us free. Jesus *came* to set us free. Yes, we will enjoy eternal life with him in heaven, but we also get to enjoy a life full of freedom during our time on earth.

Reflect

What burdens your mind today? Hand it over to Christ and claim freedom over it.

I declare that I am set free. I thank you for the freedom I find in you, Jesus. I stand firm knowing you created me to live a full life, and I speak that over myself today. Amen.

What Lies Ahead

No, dear brothers and sisters, I have not achieved it,
but I focus on this one thing: Forgetting the past
and looking forward to what lies ahead.

PHILIPPIANS 3:13 NLT

We all have to deal with baggage from our past and maybe
even our previous ways of living. It's true that old habits die
hard, and scars are often easy to spot. While Jesus can heal us
and God can use our past for his glory, we have to play our
part in it, too, which requires hard work and intentional effort.

For example, we have to learn not to worship our
problems but to worship the problem-solver. We have to
get out of the circular mindset of worry, stress, and fear and
instead direct our thoughts toward heaven. I have read the
end of the Bible, and we win, sister. God is victorious.

Reflect

Focus on what lies ahead of you today.
What are you excited about? What is God doing
through you? Share your answers with someone today.

*I shift my focus to you, Father. You are in control over the
heavens and on earth. You are good and mighty, and I know
you will use my past and my scars to glorify you. That is the
desire of my heart. Amen.*

The Devil's Lie

"God knows that when you eat from it your eyes will be opened, and you will be like God, knowing good and evil."

GENESIS 3:5 NIV

Genesis 3 tells the story of Eve in the garden of Eden, falling victim to the devil's lie that God was withholding wisdom from her and Adam when it came to the forbidden fruit. So many of us still fall victim to this same lie that God is holding out on us. It is a lie, friend. God never prevents us from obtaining or achieving that which is best for us.

God knows us better than we know ourselves because he created us, so, of course, he knows exactly what fulfills us. He guides us and warns us to protect us. His commandments are not burdensome; they are life-giving. He always wants the absolute best for us.

Reflect

What is something from God that you are waiting for? In your prayer time today, rest assured that he isn't holding out on you and praise him for his plans.

Lord, thank you for your truth. Thank you for putting your words on my heart. Thank you for wanting the best for me. I love you. Amen.

March

People of Passion

Whatever you do, work at it with all your heart,
as working for the Lord, not for human masters.

COLOSSIANS 3:23 NIV

I am a passionate person. I can't help it; I'm Italian. My friends would come over after school and hear my mom yelling before asking if they should come back another day. I would reply, "Oh, she's making us a snack. That's just how she talks!"

I believe God wants us to be people of passion, especially when it comes to our faith. We are determined and committed to Jesus, and our calling should create such a passion inside of us that everyone can see it—no matter what. We, too, will be challenged, and the devil will come at us, but we remain focused and passionate about our ministry.

Reflect

Praise Jesus that he didn't quit the cross.
What passions of yours can glorify God?

Thank you for my passions and interests, Lord. I hand over my talents to you. Use them for your glory, Jesus. Amen.

Temple of God

Don't you realize that all of you together are the temple of
God and that the Spirit of God lives in you?

1 CORINTHIANS 3:16 NLT

We need to know who we are at our core, and Scripture tells
us just that. We are the temple of God on this earth. The veil
has been torn, and there is no longer separation between God
and us. He created us, and Christ's Spirit dwells within us. We
are daughters of the heir—chosen, holy, and dearly loved.

I am God's masterpiece. He is for me, not against me. He
goes before me, beyond me, above me, and below me. I am
equipped to live out his plan for my life, which is infinitely
better than my own plan.

Reflect

Read the last paragraph of today's devotion out loud and
declare it over yourself. Believe it!

*Lord, I thank you for your Holy Spirit. I invite your power
into my life. I want to know you deeper. I want your will to be
done in my life. Amen.*

Glory of God

God, who said, "Let there be light in the darkness," has made
this light shine in our hearts so we could know the glory of
God that is seen in the face of Jesus Christ.

2 Corinthians 4:6 nlt

We see God's glory in Jesus Christ. And because Christ is
within us, we have the privilege of knowing the hope of
glory, too, my friend. Glory will burst forth in this world
because of our faith. People around us will see the hope
of Jesus because of the decisions we make every day—in
the smile we give, the encouraging word we share, and the
helping hand we offer.

We have the light of God in us, and we shine it to this
world. His love pours out of us because we are filled with
Jesus, not with ourselves. I pray for you with this godly love,
sweet sister. It is an honor and a privilege to study God's
Word together.

Reflect

Tell someone in your life what God is revealing to you
through his Word.

Thank you, Jesus, for the light you shine into my heart.
I seek you today. Amen.

Boundaries

Let your foot be seldom in your neighbor's house,
lest he have his fill of you and hate you.

PROVERBS 25:17 ESV

Ask yourself the following question: *Do I often feel over-committed, overwhelmed by my schedule, or pulled into other people's issues?* If your answer is yes, then these are indicators that you need to set better, stronger boundaries in your life.

For example, we all do better when we have a good night's rest. But if we fail to get enough sleep in any given week, then we need to set aside more time for rest the following week, set a boundary with ourselves, and commit to going to bed earlier. In the case of toxic or stressful relationships, it's easy to justify concerning patterns of behavior, but sometimes we need to set boundaries by reducing the amount of time we spend with that person or letting her go from our lives altogether.

Reflect

Consider the healthy habits and boundaries you already have in place. Celebrate those! Next, locate areas in your life that you could improve.

*Lord, you see and know all that goes on in my life.
Thank you for caring for me and for giving me the tools to
succeed and enjoy healthy relationships. Amen.*

Seasons of Faith

There is a time for everything,
and a season for every activity under the heavens.

ECCLESIASTES 3:1 NIV

If you have time today, then I encourage you to read the
entire chapter of Ecclesiastes 3, even if you're already
familiar with it. I encourage you to read it because it's rich
with wisdom. Verse 11 tells us, "He has made everything
beautiful in its time." What a promise!

What type of season are you in right now when it comes
to your faith? Are you fired up and seeing God's fingerprints
all over your day? Have you grown stale in your faith?
Perhaps you are in a season of waiting on God. Whatever
season of life we are in right now, we can be certain that God
will make it beautiful in his perfect timing.

Reflect

Identify the season you are in right now. Praise God for it
even if it's not a season you would necessarily choose.

*I thank you, Lord, for making all things beautiful in my life.
I claim that promise over my life today. Amen.*

Bright Future

Wisdom is sweet to your soul. If you find it, you will have a
bright future, and your hopes will not be cut short.

PROVERBS 24:14 NLT

Wisdom is important for us to glorify God. We need to seek
it constantly and push ourselves to the next level toward
God's purpose for us. You are worthy of significance, sweet
sister. You are worthy of all the things God has created you
for. You are worthy of asking for wisdom and believing that
you will receive his goodness and favor.

God's Word is so rich and good, but many times we
don't believe it's possible for us. I am here to tell you that it
is! Claim what is already yours. Your hopes will not be cut
short, and you will have a bright future.

Reflect

Identity five hopes that you're carrying right now.
Talk to God about them today.

*You see me, God. You know my thoughts and my hopes.
I ask for more of you in my life, Lord. Amen.*

Spiritual Fight

The thief comes only to steal and kill and destroy.

JOHN 10:10 NIV

The devil is a liar, and he will try to convince us to doubt ourselves. We fight him in a spiritual realm, friend. In our mind. In our deeds and words. In what we think and say to ourselves. He tries to speak destruction over us and attempts to sabotage any good thing coming our way by convincing us that we don't deserve it. We may want to give up at times, or we might feel as though we are failing. What are we to do?

Stand firm and be in God's Word. Spend time worshiping and talking to the Holy Spirit. We know who wins in the end, so we can walk with the swag of daughters of the King and as heirs to his throne. Remember the second part of today's verse: "I have come that they may have life, and have it to the full." In Jesus, we have a full life!

Reflect

Identify an area in your life that doesn't feel full right now. Take that to the Lord during your quiet time today.

Thank you for setting me free, Jesus.
I praise you for calling me higher. Amen.

Strong and Courageous

"Be strong and courageous. Do not be frightened,
and do not be dismayed, for the LORD your God
is with you wherever you go."

JOSHUA 1:9 ESV

My mom will often tell me to "cowgirl up," and I believe we sometimes need loved ones to remind us of that advice. We are not yet living in heaven, and on this side of the sun, we are sure to experience pain. We will go through hard times, and we won't always get everything we want or the way we want it.

We have to remember that God is ever-present with us, and he will make all things good for his glory. Trust him. Be strong and courageous.

Reflect

Imagine God's physical presence with you today. As you speak, as you walk, as you go about your day, imagine you have his love and help by your side.

*Lord, thank you for giving me your courage
and strength today. I cling to you. Amen.*

Sweet Friends

The heartfelt counsel of a friend
is as sweet as perfume and incense.

PROVERBS 27:9 NLT

To be seen and known and to share life with friends is true
joy for our souls. We cheer one another on, we are bravely
vulnerable with each other, and we serve as trustworthy
confidants to our sisters in Jesus. And it's good to invest in
the people God puts in our lives.

However, I have also learned that we need to expect
our friends to be our friends and expect Jesus to be Jesus.
In other words, we sometimes expect our friends to fill a
supernatural void in us, and that's impossible and unfair.
Our friends make life sweet, but Jesus makes our lives
satisfying. He has the answers for us. It is good to have
people come with us to the mountaintops and the gardens
in our life, but we go to those places to meet with Jesus. He
must be our focus. Always.

Reflect

Plan a hangout with one of your friends and let her know
how much her friendship means to you.

I thank you for the friends you have placed in my life, Lord.
Give me the wisdom to know how to be a better friend and
help me guide my friends to you always. Amen.

Desert Plans

In a desert land he found him, in a barren and howling waste. He shielded him and cared for him; he guarded him as the apple of his eye.

DEUTERONOMY 32:10 NIV

Over and over in the Bible, we read stories of God meeting his people in the desert in times of need. He shows up to Moses as a burning bush in the desert. He also talks to Hagar as she's running away in the desert. Praying for a desert wasteland is anything but a typical prayer request. That's because we want to be used by God, but we also want everything to be perfect. We don't want our life interrupted; we want safety, comfort, and security. We want to know the plan and details of our ministry before we boldly take that first step, but that isn't the way the Lord works.

Wherever you find yourself today, know that you are right where God wants you. Even in your suffering, even in the barren, howling waste, God is with you. He has a plan to bring you to your promised land.

Reflect

Praise God for the desert seasons in your life.

Lord, I praise you for always showing up for me in times of need. Thank you for caring for me so tenderly. Amen.

Unchanging God

> "I the LORD do not change.
> So you, the descendants of Jacob, are not destroyed."
> MALACHI 3:6 NIV

Our verse today is a great reminder for us that God is unchanging. His character is constant. He is always good, always just, and always loving. When life feels out of control, we can place our hope and rest in the knowledge that God is in control. We are guaranteed to be victorious in this life!

The Bible is full of stories of God's faithfulness. We read and hear stories of what he's done in the lives of other believers, and our faith strengthens. That's why it's important for us to reflect on all that God has done for his people. We should also reflect and worship God for all he has done for us personally. Remembering God's faithfulness brings joy to our hearts and glory to our King.

Reflect

Reflect on God's faithfulness in your life.

Thank you, Jesus, for your unwavering, unchanging nature.
Even in chaos, you are constant and true.
I worship your holy presence.

Humble Yourself

Do nothing from selfish ambition or conceit, but in humility
count others more significant than yourselves.

PHILIPPIANS 2:3 ESV

Pride can be so sneaky that we sometimes fail to recognize
when we're acting out of it. And humility is hard. When
you look up the word *humble*, the definition doesn't sound
like something we would want to strive after: "Ranking low
in a hierarchy or scale: insignificant, unpretentious." This
seems to be the opposite of what Scripture tells us since we
are encouraged to remember that we are heirs to the throne,
adopted children of the Most High.

Why should we have a low view of ourselves when
the Creator of the world concerns himself with our every
thought? In a word: Jesus. Jesus is our shining example of
humility. He doesn't have low self-esteem. He placed the
needs of others above his own, even at the cost of his life.
The first shall be last and the last shall be first.

Reflect

Find a way to put the needs of others above your own today.

*Lord, I desire to be more like Jesus. Open my eyes to any areas
of pride in my heart. I hand them over to you, Lord. Amen.*

Steadfast Love

The LORD will fulfill his purpose for me;
your steadfast love, O LORD, endures forever.
Do not forsake the work of your hands.

PSALM 138:8 ESV

Mark Twain said that "comparison is the death of joy," and research agrees. Scientific data has found that comparing yourself to others breeds envy, lowers self-confidence, compromises our ability to trust others, and can lead to depression. So why do we do it? How do we protect ourselves from the pitfalls of comparison?

I would argue that we combat thoughts or habits of comparison with the Word of God. Today's verse assures us that God has a specific purpose for each and every one of us. We sometimes become so concerned with what's happening with others that we miss out on all the things that God's hands are working out in our own lives. Remember that his love is steadfast.

Reflect

Focus today on God's steadfast love for you.
Allow him to love you.

*Thank you for your enduring, steadfast love, Jesus.
I praise you for fulfilling your purpose for me in my life.
I trust the work of your hands. Amen.*

Dangerous Mindsets

The disciples had forgotten to bring bread, except for one loaf they had with them in the boat. "Be careful," Jesus warned them. "Watch out for the yeast of the Pharisees and that of Herod."

MARK 8:14–15 NIV

Jesus warns us about two types of yeast: that of the Pharisees and of Herod. The Pharisee mindset is one of pride and arrogance. People who have this mindset hide behind rules and rituals and believe they know all of life's answers. Set in their ways, they question God and refuse to allow his Spirit to move within them.

A Herod mindset is a political spirit that capitalizes on fear and shame. Boy, do we see a lot of this in our culture today. Even back in Jesus' time, politics was a quick way to divide a group. Perhaps we are fearful of what we don't know or don't understand, but Jesus cautions us against this type of thinking. We are all included in Jesus' kingdom, so we must be careful not to divide people with our thoughts or our words.

Reflect

Consider the two types of mindsets and identify areas in your life in which you might fall into these ways of thinking.

Lord, I draw near to you today. Please make me aware of any traps that I've fallen into in my mind. I submit to you, Lord. Amen.

Joy of Salvation

Restore to me the joy of your salvation,
and uphold me with a willing spirit.

PSALM 51:12 ESV

What I found interesting as I studied this verse from God's Word is that *chara*, the Greek word for "joy," is often intertwined with *charis*, meaning "grace." Of course grace is intertwined with joy in the Word of God. It is through God's grace that he sent his Son and that we have the joy of salvation. It is through God's grace that we are forgiven. It's through his grace that we have the power of forgiveness.

We are joyful because of our salvation, and that inner joy is the faith and hope of God inside us. No person or circumstance could ever rob us of this joy. It's eternal. And even though we do not deserve God's presence and Spirit, they pour out on us fully because of his grace and love. What a beautiful display of his goodness!

Reflect

Praise God joyfully in your quiet time today.

I lift a shout of praise to heaven today, Lord. Thank you for your grace and the joy of my salvation. Amen.

Never Abandoned

The women of Bethlehem blessed Naomi:
"Praise Yahweh, who never abandoned you."
RUTH 4:14 TPT

This verse tells the happy ending to Naomi's overwhelming grief. She was convinced that God had abandoned her, leaving her without an heir to the family and their land after her husband had died. But her daughter-in-law, Ruth, eventually gave birth to a son, continuing the family of Naomi's late husband. Not only did God provide an heir for Naomi, but this boy would go on to become the grandfather to David, Israel's greatest king and an ancestor to Jesus!

God never gives up on, deserts, or abandons his people. Never. Even when he doesn't seem near, he is doing good things. When he feels far from us or we can't sense his presence, we must remember his goodness. We must fix our eyes on Jesus, our Savior, who never forsakes us.

Reflect

Thank God today for never abandoning you, even in the darkest, most challenging circumstances.

Even when I have no control and feel hopeless, I know that you will show up for me as you showed up for Naomi, Lord. Thank you for never abandoning me. Amen.

Truly

Truly my soul finds rest in God;
my salvation comes from him.

PSALM 62:1 NIV

I love the word *truly* in this verse as a launch for us today. *Truly* is a word of assurance. David, the author of the book of Psalms, isn't lying or saying the right thing just to say it. David knows it to be true and truly believes that his soul finds rest in God and that his salvation comes from God.

Our souls find rest when we spend time with our Creator, whose presence is a gift. When we go to him daily, we walk in union with him. We start to become more and more like Jesus because we are in his presence. David did this, and he was described as "a man after [God's] own heart" (Acts 13:22 NIV). Let that be our life purpose, and our souls will find rest along the way.

Reflect

Spend time with Jesus and allow your soul to rest.

You are truly my King, Lord. My soul finds rest in your presence. My salvation comes from you. Amen.

Called to Freedom

You, my brothers and sisters, were called to be free.
But do not use your freedom to indulge the flesh;
rather, serve one another humbly in love.

GALATIANS 5:13 NIV

God knows us. He made us, and he sent his Son to set us free. He has forgiven our sins, and we are seen pure and holy in the presence of all the angels and our God most high, who is more concerned with our hearts than our appearances. And thank goodness for that! I would much rather have an honest, real relationship with Jesus than the facade of one.

This freedom also empowers us to love and serve others. We love because we overflow with God's love, not simply because we feel obligated to do so. What a reason to praise, worship, and enjoy peace that no one and nothing can steal. And you know what? There is true freedom in that.

Reflect

Go the extra mile today when loving the people
God has placed in your life.

Jesus, thank you for setting me free from the chains of this world. I worship you with all my soul. I experience your freedom and lay all of my stress at your feet. Amen.

Champion-Deliverer

The Israelites, with shattered hearts, cried out to Yahweh for mercy, and he answered them by raising up a champion-deliverer to rescue them.

JUDGES 3:9 TPT

It wasn't until the Israelites were completely devastated that they cried out to the Lord for help. Enslaved by a foreign king, the Israelites finally humbled themselves, and the Lord answered their cries by giving them a new champion-deliverer.

Why is it so difficult for us to admit that we need God's help sometimes? We feel such a need for control and to rely on our own abilities that it's not until we've failed or exhausted ourselves that we turn to God. But we are to rely on the Lord first and foremost. He is merciful, and he wants us to depend on him and him alone, not ourselves. Pride has no room in his kingdom.

Reflect

What are you stubbornly trying to accomplish or work through on your own? Humble yourself before God and ask him for help instead.

Thank you for always hearing my cries, Lord.
Help me remember to rely on you in all things. Amen.

Power, Love, and Self-Control

God gave us a spirit not of fear
but of power and love and self-control.

2 TIMOTHY 1:7 ESV

Our verse today talks about the spirit that is inside each of us. I love this verse and claimed it with my Bible study girls every day during the COVID-19 pandemic. Life was intense for so many of us with work and homeschooling, and the future felt so uncertain. We all experienced the hardships of 2020 in our own ways, but I found myself clinging to this promise in 2 Timothy.

I love that self-control is included in this verse because it takes self-control to win the war inside our minds. We must not believe everything we think, and we can't allow fear to rule us. We have power, love, and self-control. Let's replace the anxious, worried spaces inside of us with God's Spirit and power.

Reflect

Choose one of the traits of the Spirit inside of you: power, love, or self-control. See how it shines through you today.

*Lord, thank you for your Spirit inside of me.
I choose you over fear. Amen.*

Done in Love

Let all that you do be done in love.

1 CORINTHIANS 16:14 ESV

"All that [we] do" is a big expectation. That includes our thoughts, our actions, our feelings, and our words—all to be done out of love. I don't know about you, ladies, but I don't always feel like being loving. I have learned, however, that feelings are merely indicators of how we are doing, but they don't make great masters. And as much as I want to be loving, I sometimes lack the necessary energy.

If you read the previous verse in 1 Corinthians, you'll read that Paul first urges them to take action: "Be watchful, stand firm in the faith, act like men, be strong" (v. 13). Then in the following verse, today's verse, Paul shifts his focus to the Corinthians' hearts. In other words, if the Corinthians don't act from a place of love, then their actions are meaningless. The same holds true for us today. We may serve well in certain areas as we go through the motions of life, but we must always come from a place of love, whether we feel like it or not.

Reflect

Do your best to live out this verse today. Let all that you do come from a place of love—even what you think and say.

Lord, you are love. I thank you for the love that I've witnessed and experienced firsthand in my life. Help me to be loving in all that I do today. Amen.

Quieted by His Love

The LORD your God is in your midst, a mighty one who will
save; he will rejoice over you with gladness; he will quiet you
by his love; he will exult over you with loud singing.

ZEPHANIAH 3:17 ESV

Zephaniah 3:17 was the first verse I memorized when I
became a follower of Jesus. I zeroed in on the last part: "He
will quiet you by his love." It felt like my life and my spirit
were in perpetual chaos before I walked with Christ. This
vision of the Lord rejoicing over me and quieting me with
his love was both comforting and beautiful.

As we allow ourselves to be quieted by his love, we become
capable of showing love and kindness to everyone he places on
our path. Let him quiet you with his love, sweet sister.

Reflect

During your quiet time today, allow the Lord to soften even
the sharpest edges of your heart.

*Lord, you are in my midst. You are mighty. You save.
I praise your name and who you are, Father. Amen.*

No Fear

There is no fear in love. But perfect love drives out fear,
because fear has to do with punishment. The one
who fears is not made perfect in love.

1 JOHN 4:18 NIV

Love casts out all fear. FEAR stands for False Expectations
Appearing Real. Fear forgets that God is in control. Fear
confuses us and breeds anxiety within our hearts and minds.

The more time we spend in God's Word, the more we
can let go of fear and let God work all things for his good.
We know what happens in the future: God wins. Let's start
leading our lives like we know the ending—because we do!

Reflect

Are we allowing God to truly love us? Are we focusing our
thoughts on God's living Spirit, or are we paralyzed by fear?
Find evidence of his love around you today.

*Lord, I want to be made perfect in your love. Help me with
my unbelief. I give you my fear and my doubts. Amen.*

Children

Jesus said, "Let the children come to me. Don't stop them! For the Kingdom of Heaven belongs to those who are like these children."

MATTHEW 19:14 NLT

Children are valued in God's kingdom. It doesn't matter to Jesus that they're younger or understand things less compared to adults. He laid his hands on them and blessed them. He tells his disciples in the chapter before, "Truly, I say to you, unless you turn and become like children, you will never enter the kingdom of heaven. Whoever humbles himself like this child is the greatest in the kingdom of heaven" (18:3–4 ESV).

There's so much we can learn from children. Their openness and humility. Their vulnerability. Their innocence. It's so easy to let our hearts harden as we become adults, but let's remember to have childlike faith, as Jesus called us to.

Reflect

How can you show childlike faith today? Ask God to help you.

I want to have childlike faith, Lord. Help me be open, vulnerable, and humble. Amen.

Strength and Gentleness

Run from all these evil things. Pursue righteousness and a godly life, along with faith, love, perseverance, and gentleness.

1 TIMOTHY 6:11 NLT

Some people hear the word *gentleness* and don't associate it with strength. If you remember from our devotion back in February, gentleness, or meekness, according to Greek-American Bible scholar Spiros Zodhiates, "does not denote outward expression or feeling, but an inward grace of the soul, calmness towards God in particular."[2] Don't you just love that definition?

Gentleness is possessing the faith, trust, and strength to submit to God's will in all circumstances. When we trust our maker, our soul is calm, and gentleness pours out of us. And we have every reason to trust our sovereign, mighty God. I hope that after today, we think of strength when we think of gentleness.

Reflect

Think of a challenge you're facing in life today. Place your trust in God and surrender to his will so that you can possess calmness through it.

Lord, I pursue a gentle spirit. Thank you for giving me faith and rest. Amen.

---

2   Spiros Zodhiates, *The Complete Word Study Dictionary: New Testament* (Chattanooga: AMG Publishers, 1994).

Prepare for Action

Preparing your minds for action, and being sober-minded,
set your hope fully on the grace that will be brought to you
at the revelation of Jesus Christ.

1 PETER 1:13 ESV

We are reminded by our verse today that we place our hope in
the grace of Jesus, which gives us salvation, peace, joy, strength,
hope, and love. This same verse also calls us to prepare our
minds for action and to have sound minds. To have a sound
mind requires self-control and is a fruit of the Holy Spirit. That
means that our minds become more and more set apart as we
spend time focusing on the power of God.

We control what our ears hear, what our eyes see, and
where our minds go. That's why we must take hold of our
minds and claim power over them. We can't let them wander
to worry but must train them to focus on the Lord.

Reflect

Pay attention to what you think about today.
Be mindful when your thoughts start to wander.

*I set my mind on you today, Jesus. Help me prepare my mind
to understand your truths and to make them a reality,
full of your power, in my life. Amen.*

The Truth

Jesus said to the Jews who had believed him, "If you abide in my word, you are truly my disciples, and you will know the truth, and the truth will set you free."

JOHN 8:31–32 ESV

The truth is that we struggle with the truth, especially as our world and culture constantly tempt us to fall away from it. This struggle, however, isn't new. In Genesis, the devil, disguised as a snake, whispers lies to Eve in the garden of Eden. Here, the devil is described as cunning, and I would say that he hasn't changed much. Even today we sometimes believe lies without even knowing they're lies.

We can come against the lies we believe if we stay in God's Word and focus on the truth. His Word and believing it set us free. Some of you are reading this and feeling uncomfortable at the mere mention of the devil. See how cunning he truly is?

Reflect

What lies do you believe about yourself? Call them out and speak truth over yourself today. You are a beloved, cherished daughter of the King.

I want to live in the truth, Lord. Speak to me through your Word. Amen.

Receive Power

"You will receive power when the Holy Spirit has come upon you, and you will be my witnesses in Jerusalem and in all Judea and Samaria, and to the end of the earth."

ACTS 1:8 ESV

In the Bible, we don't read of God's people praying for him to retreat. They pray for his strength and boldness. They say, "Yes, Lord!" That's because God is powerful, and he promises that same power lives in each of us.

Many of us carry this mentality that we should beg God in our prayer lives, seeming to forget that we have the power of the Holy Spirit inside us. We are called to be God's witnesses to the ends of the earth. Others should feel the power of your prayers. *You* should feel the power of your prayers. Be bold today in your prayer life, sister!

Reflect

Have you ever prayed for the power of God to be revealed to you in your life? Pray for the presence of God today and meditate on his power.

Lord, thank you for being so powerful. Thank you for your Holy Spirit living in me. I pray that you use me for your glory, Jesus. Amen.

Love and Consideration

Let us consider how to stir up one another
to love and good works.

HEBREWS 10:24 ESV

I love the word *consider* in this verse. It's easy to overlook, but everyone is created differently, so it makes sense that we should love one another differently. The way one person likes to receive love may be completely different from the way someone else likes to be loved. It's our responsibility to truly get to know the people we are in community with so that we can consider how best to encourage them.

This verse also reminds us of the importance of fellowship in our lives. We are called to spur one another on and to share our lives with each other. Joy can be found in crying with a friend and laughing with a friend. God will place people in our lives, and it is our job to invest in those friendships and be mindful to sincerely consider them.

Reflect

When was the last time you enjoyed the body of Christ?
Consider how you can stir up a friend today
so that she feels loved.

*I thank you for the power and joy of community, Lord.
I pray that I thoughtfully consider each of my friends
so that I can love them well. Amen.*

Find Rest

"Come to me, all you who are weary and burdened, and I will give you rest. Take my yoke upon you and learn from me, for I am gentle and humble in heart, and you will find rest for your souls. For my yoke is easy and my burden is light."

MATTHEW 11:28–30 NIV

Busyness is sold as desirable these days, as if it's something to attain. We're asked, "How are you doing?" We reply, "Oh, I'm so busy. Things are crazy." Then we're praised with something like, "Oh, good for you." But God did not create us to live life this way. Christ tells us that he wants us to have a full life. An abundant life. He says that we're called to be set free. His yolk is easy and light.

What are you carrying right now that you were not created to carry? Perhaps it's stress, anger, worry, or fear. What do you need rest from in your head and in your heart? Remember that you were not made to drag it around with you everywhere you go. God wants you to rest it in his capable hands.

Reflect

Answer the questions in today's devotion in a real and honest conversation with Jesus. Let your soul be at rest today.

Lord, I thank you for your capable hands and gentle, humble heart. Help me learn from you and find rest for my soul. Amen.

In All Situations

Hell and destruction are never full;
so the eyes of man are never satisfied.

PROVERBS 27:20 KJV

This verse seems sad and dark to focus on for the day, but I promise you that we can find encouragement and wisdom in it. We live in a culture and a time in history that is overwhelmingly dark. Dissatisfaction is practically encouraged, so the idea that we can live in perpetual contentment seems unattainable, but it isn't.

Contentment in all situations is possible because in all situations, we have the hope of Jesus. When we permit self-pity or dissatisfaction to live in our minds, they are never quenched. Instead, we must shift our focus off of ourselves, off of the broken world we live in, and on to the Lord. He gives us satisfaction and contentment in all circumstances.

Reflect

Identify areas in your life in which you're unsatisfied
and invite Jesus to work on them with you.

*You have given me a spirit of power and a sound mind. I want to be full of peace and contentment in every situation. I want to be content in every season of my life because I know you are making all things good in all situations. I trust you.
I submit to you. Amen.*

April

Cast Your Anxiety

Cast all your anxiety on him because he cares for you.

1 Peter 5:7 niv

To be completely transparent, I never struggled with anxiety in a real way until the COVID-19 pandemic. I felt the weight of the world every day. I found it difficult to breathe at night, and I started experiencing eye-twitching, heart racing, and a feeling like everything was totally out of my control. I brought my concerns to the Lord, who revealed that it was anxiety.

My mental state became healthier once I started spending more time in his Word and in his presence, and my eye twitch even went away. I scrolled less on Instagram and avoided going down rabbit holes online. I made the decision to protect my mind, laying my cares on Jesus instead. We all experience stress and worry differently, and trust me when I say that I know how blessed I am that this approach worked for me when millions of people require medication or therapy. There's no shame in seeking help, whether that's from the Lord, a psychiatrist, a therapist, or a combination of all three. I support you, sister!

Reflect

Share your mental state with God today.

Thank you for caring for me and carrying my burdens. I have the hope of your beauty sewn into my soul, Jesus. Amen.

The Lord Is Close

The LORD is close to the brokenhearted
and saves those who are crushed in spirit.

PSALM 34:18 NIV

Our beautiful verse today promises that God is close to us when we feel broken. He saves our crushed spirit and desires an open, honest relationship with us. We must be honest about the areas in which we are broken and submit those to Christ in a sincere, intimate way.

Acknowledge your pain and bring it to the Lord. He can handle it, and there is no safer place for our pain and sorrow than in the throne room of Christ. Trade in your brokenness for God's plan over your life.

Reflect

What is an area that you are still holding on to that is broken? Submit that to the Lord today.

Lord, thank you for allowing me to bring my hurt and brokenness to you. Thank you for seeing me and drawing near to me in times of joy and in times of pain. You are always there for me. I love you. Amen.

Let It Go

Beloved, never avenge yourselves, but leave it to
the wrath of God, for it is written, "Vengeance is mine,
I will repay, says the Lord."

ROMANS 12:19 ESV

I love that this verse starts with "Beloved." Letting go and
forgiving others doesn't come naturally to most of us. We
want justice. But the word *beloved* reminds us that when
the Lord instructs us to act against our human nature, it's
because he loves us. He's guiding us, his beloved children. He
does not withhold from us; he gives us sound advice.

We don't have to put ourselves in the position to get
hurt again, but we do need to let things go for our own
sake. God will avenge us as he sees fit. Release the burden of
offense from yourself and submit it to God, trusting that he
will work all things out. If you've done this before, then you
know how freeing it feels.

Reflect

Let it go and let God avenge you.

*Lord, I pray for the areas of unforgiveness in my heart.
I want to be released from the bitterness I hold within.
Help me to forgive and move forward today. Amen.*

Love More, Judge Less

You have no excuse, O man, every one of you who judges.
For in passing judgment on another you condemn yourself,
because you, the judge, practice the very same things.

ROMANS 2:1 ESV

We are quick to judge, but we must remember that is neither our duty nor our talent. We are actually bad at it, and Paul goes so far as to write that we have no excuse to judge. My pastor once said. "God waits to judge us until we die, so what makes us think that we have the right to judge people when we don't know the whole story?"

We are called to love and to leave the judging to Jesus. Judging others is indicative of a prideful heart, so we must humble ourselves. When we come to understand that God created, loves, and pursues everyone, then we can love more and judge less.

Reflect

Do your best not to judge anyone today, and if you do,
replace your judgment with love.

Lord, you are the judge and jury of creation. Help me to recognize when I'm being judgmental. My desire is to love everyone you place in my path. Amen.

Abba

Because we are his children, God has sent the Spirit of his
Son into our hearts, prompting us to call out, "Abba, Father."

GALATIANS 4:6 NLT

What a privilege it is to have the Holy Spirit living inside of
us. Every believer has the power of the Spirit inside of them.
His presence within our hearts is both the guarantee and the
proof that we have been made "children of God" and joint
heirs with Christ.

The intimacy we can have with God is shown with this
idea of crying out, "Abba, Father." Jesus famously called out
to God in Aramaic, his native language, using these very
words in the garden of Gethsemane (see Mark 14:36).

Reflect

Do you feel like God's daughter? Do you feel comfortable
enough to talk to him in your "native language" as the
person you truly are? Not using a "prayer voice" or fancy
words but speaking just as you are. Talk to him today in
your own native language.

*Thank you for the dwelling of your Holy Spirit inside of my
heart. I praise your holy name. Amen.*

The Way

Jesus answered, "I am the way and the truth and the life.
No one comes to the Father except through me."

JOHN 14:6 NIV

As Jesus prepared for the cross, he gave his followers the
foundations of his message at the last supper. He encourages
us to love one another and declare him as Lord. He tells
us he is the way and the truth, and we cannot know God
without knowing him. He makes way for us to have a
fulfilled life on earth and an eternal life in heaven.

It's easy to be led astray by this world, as we're constantly
hearing lies, even from our own hearts and thoughts. But
when we fix our gaze on Jesus, we can recognize the lies
because we become armed with the truth of Christ. Living
in the truth gives us life—the life Jesus created for us—a life
overflowing with love.

Reflect

How do the people around you know that Jesus is your way,
your truth, and your life? Demonstrate that in your life today.

*Lord, thank you for being the truth that reigns in my heart.
May I be a beacon of your love. Amen.*

He Understands

About three in the afternoon Jesus cried out in a loud voice,
"Eli, Eli, lema sabachthani?" (which means "My God,
my God, why have you forsaken me?").

MATTHEW 27:46 NIV

Jesus is calling out to God, not as God but as man. The fullness
of the Godhead still had dwelled inside of Jesus until the
moment we read of in our verse today. Because God cannot
look on sin. Jesus took all of our darkness, which separated
him from God. And once that happened, Jesus felt abandoned.
Jesus was fully God and fully man, so he understands
our nature, our humanity, because he, too, was human.
He has felt all of the pain, stress, and loneliness that
accompanies the human experience, and he understands
our sorrow because he experienced it firsthand. He paid
the ultimate price for us, and we praise his holy name. How
blessed we are to serve a God of power and justice who
simultaneously overflows with such mercy and love.

Reflect

Identify moments in your own life when you have felt
forsaken by God. Talk to God about that today.

Lord, thank you for understanding and never forsaking me.
You sent your beloved Son to pay the price for my salvation,
and I am eternally grateful beyond words. Amen.

Forgiveness

> "When you stand praying, if you hold anything against anyone, forgive them, so that your Father in heaven may forgive you your sins."
>
> MARK 11:25 NIV

Prayer transforms us and helps us shine God's glory, but praying for someone we despise or who has caused us pain or harm is super hard. I know this firsthand. When we carry unforgiveness in our hearts, we alienate God from that part of ourselves, and guess what fills that gap? Darkness. The Enemy. Bitterness. Anger. Mistrust. When we offer up forgiveness, light enters into that dark space immediately.

Forgiving someone doesn't make their offense acceptable or okay, but it does free us from the burden of carrying it around. If there is darkness in us because of unforgiveness, we can submit that to God, and he will fill that darkness with light. Forgiveness is the work of the Holy Spirit, friend, and it's healing.

Reflect

Forgive someone who has hurt you. If you're struggling with doing so, that's okay. Talk to God about it.

Thank you for giving me your Spirit of love, Lord. I don't want to harbor unforgiveness in my soul; I want to forgive. Amen.

Raised from the Dead

What is the immeasurable greatness of his power toward us who believe, according to the working of his great might that he worked in Christ when he raised him from the dead and seated him at his right hand in the heavenly places.

EPHESIANS 1:19–20 ESV

Jesus conquered death. He was dead but came back to earth alive, and his resurrection is the basis of our faith. The very disciples who saw him die also saw his risen body, and many of them died for their faith. These truths have permanently changed humanity and the course of eternity.

Currently, Jesus is seated at the right hand of God and constantly intercedes on our behalf. As the accuser declares our darkness, Jesus claims us as his. Oh, what power and love come from the cross. Whatever darkness uses for destruction, God turns into life.

Reflect

Set aside time today to think about the story of the cross. Praise God for conquering death. Don't let the familiarity of the story rob you of its wonder and power.

Jesus, I praise your holy name. You have risen from the dead, and I declare you as Lord. Amen.

Heavy Hearts

Why, my soul, are you downcast? Why so disturbed within me? Put your hope in God, for I will yet praise him, my Savior and my God.

PSALM 42:5 NIV

I remember a time when I received bad news, and I was so sad that I sat in my car, parked in my driveway, and cried. I know we've all been there—where we know that Jesus is in control and yet we still hurt because our hopes have been dashed. But as I cried, today's beautiful psalm flooded my mind. It reminded me that we can't hide our sorrow from Jesus and that God wants to comfort us when we're sad.

Even when our souls are downcast, we will praise him. Even when things aren't going our way, we will yet have faith in God. We won't let sorrow draw us away from Jesus. We will draw near to Christ even when we feel like pushing him away.

Reflect

Think of something in your life that's challenging or disheartening to you, then declare this truth out loud: "Even though this is happening in my life right now, I will yet praise him."

For I will yet have faith even when I don't see or feel you, Lord. My hope is in you. Even when my heart is heavy, I will praise your holy name. Amen.

Unforgiveness

Anyone you forgive, I also forgive. And what I have forgiven—if there was anything to forgive—I have forgiven in the sight of Christ for your sake, in order that Satan might not outwit us. For we are not unaware of his schemes.

2 CORINTHIANS 2:10–11 NIV

In today's verses, Paul warns us of the dangers of unforgiveness. When we carry unforgiveness around with us, then we make ourselves susceptible to Satan, who might "outwit" us by dividing us. He wants us to be bitter and angry with each other because, if God's people are divided, then we're not doing his work, which is exactly what the devil wants. We have to be on guard and avoid gossiping, harboring anger, or inviting stress into our lives. Even when someone hurts us, we're accountable for our actions.

But as Paul wisely notes, we know Satan's schemes, and we have the tools and the power to set ourselves free from the negative effects of unforgiveness. We have to let go of that pain and surrender it to Christ so that he may use it for his glory.

Reflect

Be aware that Satan might try to outwit you and draw you further from the Lord today and in the coming weeks.

I cling to you, Jesus. Your will and plans for my life are the best, and I submit all I have to you, Lord. Amen.

Watch in Hope

I watch in hope for the LORD, I wait for God my Savior;
my God will hear me.

MICAH 7:7 NIV

I love how the first focus of this verses reads, "I watch in hope." That sounds active and expectant to me. That doesn't sound like a weak faith but a bold, courageous, powerful declaration of faith.

We wait on God. We don't settle for less than what he has planned for us because we know that he hears our prayers. We know that he is mighty, good, and faithful, so we place our hope in him. Let's stand guard against hopelessness in our hearts and instead watch in hope, expecting great things.

Reflect

Read this verse aloud with conviction. Declare it as your own.

Lord, I watch in hope. I know you hear my cries, and I am confident and hopeful that you are doing mighty work. Thank you. I praise you. Amen.

Fruit of the Spirit

The Holy Spirit produces this kind of fruit in our lives: love, joy, peace, patience, kindness, goodness, faithfulness, gentleness, and self-control.

GALATIANS 5:22–23 NLT

The fruit of our life is all of the good that people can observe in us, and all of it comes from the Spirit of the Lord. I want the fruit of my life to be good. I want my marriage to be a source of peace and joy to my family and everyone around us. I want people to leave my home feeling loved and full of kindness after hanging out with me.

A life marked by the fruit of the Spirit is within reach for all of us, and it's how we were designed to live.

Reflect

Memorize all nine fruits of the Spirit
and select one to exude today.

Lord, I want the overflow of my spirit to be love, joy, peace, patience, kindness, goodness, faithfulness, gentleness, and self-control. Amen.

Overflowing Hope

May the God of hope fill you with all joy and peace as you trust in him, so that you may overflow with hope by the power of the Holy Spirit.

ROMANS 15:13 NIV

In today's verse, Paul reminds us to focus on the God of hope. That means we need to trust in his goodness, his will for us, and his promises over our life. Trusting him fully brings us peace, and we must have peace *with* God before we can enjoy the peace *of* God.

Do you have hope, joy, and peace because you placed your trust in God? Perhaps you are doubting him in a certain area of your life. Maybe, like Eve in the garden of Eden, you feel like God is holding out on you. While we know we shouldn't question or doubt him, our fear gets the best of us sometimes. Remember that he is the God of hope. Focus on his love.

Reflect

Place your trust in God today. Visualize yourself handing over everything to him—your stressors, your dreams, your fears, and your desires.

Lord, my hope is in you. I am full of doubt at times, but I want to overflow with peace and joy that only your Holy Spirit can bring into my life. Amen.

A Pure Heart

The aim of our charge is love that issues from a pure heart
and a good conscience and a sincere faith.

1 TIMOTHY 1:5 ESV

The focus of our day today is love, sweet sister. We are called to love from a pure heart, a good conscience, and a sincere faith. We risk losing those beautiful qualities when we defile our hearts, and we defile our hearts when we fail to recognize and avoid sin, allowing the world to convince us that it's mere weakness. The truth is that sin is sin.

What we listen to matters. What our eyes see matters. What our minds think matters. And the words that come out of our mouths matter. We are largely in control of each of those things, and all these seemingly little moments and choices are connected.

Reflect

In your personal life, do the people who aren't yet believers notice or remark on how different you are by the words you speak and the things you do? Consider how you can be more disciplined in your thoughts, words, or actions to separate yourself from the world and draw closer to God.

*Lord, I desire to love from a pure heart and a sincere faith.
Reveal to me the areas in my heart that I need
to surrender to you today. Amen.*

Patience

The Lord is not slow in keeping his promise, as some
understand slowness. Instead he is patient with you, not
wanting anyone to perish, but everyone to come to repentance.

2 PETER 3:9 NIV

The Greek word for "patience" is *makrothumia*, and
according to *Strong's Expanded Exhaustive Concordance of
the Bible*, it also means "endurance, constancy, steadfastness,
and perseverance."[3] I love this definition because I don't
consider myself a patient person, but this definition gives me
hope. When I want to react and express my impatience, I try
to choose to restrain myself to demonstrate patience.

I don't know about you, but I never realized that
patience and salvation went hand in hand. God is so patient
with us, and it should encourage us to demonstrate that
same patience to those around us.

Reflect

Demonstrate patience today.

*Lord, thank you for your patience with me and for constantly
pursuing me. I am so grateful for your grace and love.
I worship you, Lord. Amen.*

---

3   Strong, *Strong's Expanded Exhaustive Concordance of the
Bible*, #3115.

Kindness

As God's chosen people, holy and dearly loved, clothe
yourselves with compassion, kindness, humility,
gentleness and patience.

COLOSSIANS 3:12 NIV

The Greek word for "kindness" is *cherestotes,* which means,
"the genuine desire of a believer to treat others gently, just
as the Lord treats him."[4] *Cherestotes* "is the grace which
pervades the whole nature, mellowing all which would
be harsh and austere…*cherestotes* is a tender heart and a
nurturing spirit."[5]

I want to focus on the first definition of kindness as
gentleness, "as the Lord treats [us]." See, we tend to focus on
the power or the judgment of God, but it's equally important
to praise his gentleness. Chances are that we'll come across
someone today who needs to be treated gently. Choose to be a
source of kindness and treat him or her as the Lord treats us.

Reflect

Be extra kind and gentle to others today. Make it a habit.

*Lord, soften me. Give me your nurturing Spirit and eyes to see
your people who are in need of a kind word or gesture today.
Amen.*

---

4   Strong, *Strong's Expanded Exhaustive Concordance of the
    Bible,* #5544.
5   Zodhiates, *The Complete Word Study Dictionary,* 1482.

Good and Faithful Servant

"Well done, good and faithful servant! You have been faithful
with a few things; I will put you in charge of many things.
Come and share your master's happiness!"

MATTHEW 25:23 NIV

When we cross the threshold of this world and enter into
the throne room, Jesus claims us as his. Out of his grace and
mercy, he'll consider us his good and faithful servants for
running toward him on this earth. How we long to embrace
him and feel his love overwhelm our souls.

Our days are to be filled with good acts out of love
for our King. The verse continues, and how does it end?
So sweetly. "Come," he says, "and share your master's
happiness!"

Reflect

Share in the happiness of the Lord today. See your life
through the lens of Jesus and let his heart be yours.

*Lord, thank you for your grace, mercy, and love.
I am overwhelmed by your goodness. Amen.*

God's Handiwork

We are God's handiwork, created in Christ Jesus to do good works, which God prepared in advance for us to do.

EPHESIANS 2:10 NIV

God calls us to be his handiwork, his works of art. He designed and created us with unique skills and a specific purpose—for *his* purposes. Nothing is random about our talents and passions, and his plans for us unfold every day. We need to see ourselves from this perspective instead of picking ourselves apart for our shortcomings. We are God's masterpieces.

Our good works don't give us salvation; only Jesus can do that, but they give us a sense of purpose and fulfillment. We can accept Jesus, but if we aren't using our God-given talents to glorify the Lord, then we won't feel fulfilled.

Reflect

Look for opportunities for God to use you today.

Lord, I praise you for the way you created me.
I know I am not perfect, but I am yours. Amen.

Royal Priesthood

You are a chosen people, a royal priesthood, a holy nation,
God's special possession, that you may declare the praises
of him who called you out of darkness into his wonderful
light. Once you were not a people, but now you are the
people of God; once you had not received mercy,
but now you have received mercy.

1 PETER 2:9–10 NIV

My husband is supportive and totally believes in me. I have
found myself taking steps of boldness in ways I would never
dream of because of his support and belief in me. Having
that support encourages me to step with confidence into
the woman Jesus created me to be. We all have that same
support in Jesus.

You are God's special possession. His chosen. His child.
You are holy. What an honor and a privilege to have that as
part of your identity!

Reflect

Remember who God says you are. Receive his mercy today
and step into the greatness he has destined for you.

*Lord, thank you for loving me. I declare praise
for calling me into the light. You are my King. Amen.*

Trustworthy

> Your kingdom is an everlasting kingdom, and your
> dominion endures through all generations. The LORD is
> trustworthy in all he promises and faithful in all he does.
>
> PSALM 145:13 NIV

Our faith can either be based on who God is or what God does. And even though the world is full of heavy heartbreak and things that don't always go our way, God is faithful and trustworthy. We must always remember who he is: a kind God full of grace and mercy. He is a God of love, kindness, and gentleness, and he never changes. We can't allow our faith to waver.

God has placed us all in this moment in time, in this time of our lives with our present circumstances, talents, and passions, for a reason. The Lord is faithful in all that he does, and as today's verse reminds us, his kingdom is everlasting, and his dominion endures through all generations.

Reflect

What promise from God are you struggling to fully trust him with? Give him that trust today.

*Lord, you are trustworthy. You abound in love and
faithfulness. I trust you, Lord. Amen.*

God's Kindness

When the kindness and love of God our Savior appeared, he
saved us, not because of righteous things we had done, but
because of his mercy. He saved us through the washing of
rebirth and renewal by the Holy Spirit, whom he poured out
on us generously through Jesus Christ our Savior, so that,
having been justified by his grace, we might become heirs
having the hope of eternal life.

TITUS 3:4–7 NIV

Today's Scripture passage is rich with hope and beauty, and I
want to focus on the beginning of the verse that talks about
God's kindness to us. The verse promises that everyone in
Christ is saved because of Jesus, whom God sent, because
God is kind and loving. His kindness overflows out of him
and into us so that we, too, can overflow with kindness.

God's transformative grace is so powerful that we have
the hope of eternal life in him. We are saved because of his
kindness. We have so much to praise God for today!

Reflect

Reread today's Scripture piece by piece, taking the time to
fully grasp and appreciate everything it reveals.

*Lord, I praise you. I praise you for your grace, Jesus, and the
Holy Spirit. Thank you for your kindness and love. Amen.*

Faithfulness

Without faith it is impossible to please God, because anyone who comes to him must believe that he exists and that he rewards those who earnestly seek him.

HEBREWS 11:6 NIV

In Greek, faithfulness is *pistis*, meaning, "conviction, belief in the truth, veracity, reality."[6] To sum it up, faithfulness means to believe in the reality of God and what he can and will do. The degree of our faithfulness correlates with how we regard God's faithfulness. That is, what we perceive from Jesus is what we receive from Jesus.

It's easy to miss out on God's faithfulness if we become impatient. That is where patience and faithfulness intersect. But we need to remember that the impossible is God's domain. He can accomplish miracles that we can only imagine, and to live in the reality of his goodness, power, and glory pleases him. As we faithfully pursue Jesus, our Father takes great delight. What a beautiful and humbling idea that our faith brings our Lord joy.

Reflect

Declare a bold faith in your heart. Earnestly seek God however that looks for you today.

Lord, I have faith in you, and I seek you. Amen.

---

6   Strong, *Strong's Expanded Exhaustive Concordance of the Bible*, #4102.

Delight in the Lord

Take delight in the LORD, and he will give you
the desires of your heart.

PSALM 37:4 NIV

Did you hear the promise in today's verse? God knows the desires of our hearts and gives them to us! That's not to say that he's a genie in a bottle; rather, he knows and wants what's best for us, and he wants our hearts to align with his will.

When we spend time with Jesus, our hearts start to change. We become more generous and more easily moved by the Spirit. We choose to spend our time with uplifting people, and we become more sensitive to dark acts, words, and motives. Jesus' presence not only changes us, but it also satisfies us and brings us joy. When we meditate on the goodness of God's love, grace, and mercy, it deposits peace into our soul. We delight in the Lord!

Reflect

Have you found joy in the presence of God?
Delight in the Lord today.

Lord, you are my great reward.
Knowing you is my heart's desire. Amen.

Crown of Righteousness

I have fought the good fight, I have finished the race, I have kept the faith. Henceforth there is laid up for me the crown of righteousness, which the Lord, the righteous judge, will award to me on that day, and not only to me but also to all who have loved his appearing.

2 TIMOTHY 4:7–8 ESV

While imprisoned, Paul wrote the letter that became 2 Timothy, and he wrote it for his spiritual son. Although he's certain he will be killed for his faith, Paul's words are incredibly encouraging. His situation could not be bleaker, but he is full of faith, hope, and inspiration.

Yes, we see evil and darkness around us, but we believe in God, and we keep our faith in Jesus. We draw near to God even when our hearts break or our future seems uncertain because his peace surpasses our understanding. We have faith in our Creator because he has the crown of righteousness in store for us.

Reflect

Do you feel that you, like Paul, are fighting the good fight? Why or why not?

Lord, I trust you. I am here to fight the good fight. Help me with my unbelief. I am yours. Amen.

Heavenly Realms

God raised us up with Christ and seated us with him in the
heavenly realms in Christ Jesus, in order that in the coming
ages he might show the incomparable riches of his grace,
expressed in his kindness to us in Christ Jesus.

EPHESIANS 2:6–7 NIV

Our Scripture today was written by Paul, who is so
convinced that God seats us in the heavenly realms with
Jesus that he writes as if it has already happened. He assumes
it's simply a matter of time, as certain as the sun will rise
tomorrow.

I also want us to appreciate the idea that God expresses
his kindness to us through Jesus Christ. Grace is God's
gesture of kindness to us, and because of it, we are saved
and called to lead lives marked by joy and freedom, starting
today and for eternity.

Reflect

Because of the grace in your life, intentionally overflow
with God's kindness to those around you.

Lord, I praise you for the things I cannot begin to understand.
To be seated with you in the heavenly realms is an
overwhelming thought that brings me to my knees.
Your kindness and love are such gifts to my soul.
I love you, Lord. Amen.

Follow His Steps

My feet have closely followed his steps;
I have kept to his way without turning aside.

JOB 23:11 NIV

Our verse today comes from the words of Job. Job was a blessed man who lost everything: his children, his income, and his health. Yet he declares amid his hardships that his feet have closely followed the Lord. I like to imagine him walking so closely behind God that Job's shoes are full of the dust that God kicked up.

It is often in the middle of hardships and uncertainty that we want to turn away from God. When everything seems to make no sense, that is when our faith truly matters. We can either put God on display or ourselves. We can trust Jesus and allow him to shine, or we can try to take control and work from a place of fear. Walk so closely to Jesus through every season that your feet, like Job's, are dusty from his path.

Reflect

How do you handle times of hardship? Do you turn away from God or turn toward him?

Jesus, I pray for confidence in my faith, like Job's. My heart's desire is to follow you and your ways and not turn from you. Amen.

Lady in Waiting

"Your relative Elizabeth in her old age has also conceived a son,
and this is the sixth month with her who was called barren."

LUKE 1:36 ESV

Have you ever found yourself in a season of waiting?
Elizabeth prayed for a child, but month after month and year
after year, Elizabeth did not become a mom. Can you relate
in your own way? I know I can. When we're in a season of
waiting, we can choose to trust God or try to control things
ourselves.

Trusting God doesn't mean sitting around and waiting
for the seas to part simply because you believe in him.
Trusting God is a posture of our hearts; it's feeling rest in our
souls even in seasons of waiting. We read in our verse today
that Elizabeth's patience and eventual pregnancy encouraged
Mary's faith. As we wait, we can still encourage our friends
and loved ones. Like Elizabeth, God may use our waiting for
his glory.

Reflect

How can you be a source of encouragement
during a season of waiting?

Lord, you are God even in the seasons of waiting.
I know you are faithful and good, and I trust you. Amen.

Boldness

Ananias departed and entered the house. And laying his hands on him he said, "Brother Saul, the Lord Jesus who appeared to you on the road by which you came has sent me so that you may regain your sight and be filled with the Holy Spirit."

ACTS 9:17 ESV

Ananias had a vision from God to go to Saul and pray for him. Saul was a dangerous man who had murdered believers, many of whom were probably personal friends of Ananias. Imagine the fear and doubt Ananias must have felt to obey God's calling.

Our relationship with God always requires action, a response. He wants our boldness and availability so that he can use us, and he calls us to step out of our comfort zones and trust him. It doesn't always end with the blind recovering their sight, but we can rest assured that it will end with us one step closer to Jesus, which is where we always want to be. Let's be bold, sister! Let's make ourselves available so that Jesus calls on us.

Reflect

Listen carefully to what God is calling you to do today.

I am yours, Lord. Use me today. Amen.

I AM

God said to Moses, "I am who i am." And he said, "Say this
to the people of Israel: 'I am has sent me to you.'"

EXODUS 3:14 ESV

Moses asked God for his name, and God gave him a
meaningful reply. He told Moses that he has no beginning
and no end. As humans, we exist within the construct of
time. That is, we have a beginning and an end to our stay on
earth. God, however, exists outside of time. He is eternal,
meaning he exists now, in the past, and in the future.

God is self-existent, and his nature has been and always
will be the same. He is the Rock of our salvation. He is
Alpha and Omega, so we can trust that he knows what he's
doing. Even when we don't understand or would do things
differently, we can enjoy peace because we know God sits on
the throne—forever.

Reflect

Meditate on the grandness of God today.

*Lord, you are who you are. I praise you for your consistency
and power. You are mighty, faithful, and good. I trust you
with my concerns and my future. Amen.*

May

All Things

In him all things were created: things in heaven and on earth, visible and invisible, whether thrones or powers or rulers or authorities; all things have been created through him and for him. He is before all things, and in him all things hold together.

COLOSSIANS 1:16–17 NIV

Our flawed human nature is prone to selfishness, and it's easy to assume everything was created for us. And then, when things inevitably don't go our way, we wonder, *Why did this happen to me? Where are you, God?* The answer is found in today's verses, which declare God's glory.

Everything was made by God and for God. He is before all things and in all things, and because of him, everything holds together. We trust in Jesus when our circumstances are unfavorable or don't make sense or are not working according to our own timelines. We trust that God, who is good, faithful, and mighty, is in control and working all things for our good and his glory. We must push aside our pride and self-obsession and focus on our Creator, who sits on the throne.

Reflect

Declare these two verses out loud with conviction.

You created everything that I see and don't see, Lord.
I praise your holy name. Amen.

Of the World

Do not love the world or the things in the world. If anyone
loves the world, the love of the Father is not in him.

1 JOHN 2:15 ESV

It seems that it's easy to get offended now more than ever.
One scroll on social media will reveal an offensive post
from a cousin's friend's boyfriend. We should be concerned
about things of eternal value, not the agenda of what the
world deems worthy or which values the world happens to
be pushing down our throats on any given day. Instead, we
want a kingdom-focused mindset.

We have to be intentional about training our thoughts
to focus on Jesus. We must operate from a place of love,
especially when we don't want to, and not become easily
offended. We must put in the daily practice of communing
with Jesus so that our souls remain connected with him.

Reflect

How can you practice a kingdom-focused mentality daily
as opposed to holding a worldly point of view?

*Lord, I want to be concerned with the things that have value to
you. Open my eyes and help me be kingdom focused. Amen.*

In Christ

If anyone is in Christ, the new creation has come:
The old has gone, the new is here!

2 CORINTHIANS 5:17 NIV

Today is a fresh, new day, and this verse powerfully reminds us that we are transformed and born again in Christ. We view those who are in Christ as whole new creations. The shame of yesterday has no place in our hearts today. God's purpose for our life replaces the old agendas, dreams, lifestyle, and everything else. The old way of death and sin is gone, and our life blossoms into love and eternity.

Instead, we focus on serving the Lord with gladness and living in the power of the Holy Spirit. When we believe in Jesus, we enter an eternal family of believers. We are no longer slaves to this world but heirs to the King. Oh, what a beautiful promise, sweet friend.

Reflect

Spend time today thinking about the ways you
have become a new creation thanks to Jesus.
Thank him for the transformation.

I am made new because of you, Jesus.
I thank you, Lord. Amen.

Omniscient

Call to me and I will answer you, and will tell you great and hidden things that you have not known.

JEREMIAH 33:3 ESV

One of God's many amazing characteristics is his omniscience. To be omniscient is to be all knowing. In a way, it's unsurprising that he knows all because he made all. He has infinite awareness, understanding, and insight. It is important for us to truly know this down to our bones. He doesn't make mistakes, and he doesn't forget about us. He is in control, and he knows what he's doing.

In today's verse, God promises us that he will answer when we call on him for understanding. God will tell us our purpose, who to marry, who to pursue friendships with, and who to be cautious with. God will give us wisdom—his wisdom—if we ask.

Reflect

Ask God for wisdom to understand something
that feels concerning or uncertain.

Lord, you are all knowing. I yearn for wisdom in my life. Reveal to me your wisdom and guide my decisions. Amen.

Transferred

He has delivered us from the domain of darkness and transferred us to the kingdom of his beloved Son, in whom we have redemption, the forgiveness of sins.

COLOSSIANS 1:13–14 ESV

This world will entice us and lie to our spirits, but we have been delivered from the domain of darkness and transferred to the kingdom of Christ. The kingdom of God is a spiritual kingdom. It exists now, in our reality today, and it exists in the future. God's kingdom calls for patience when we are in a rush, forgiveness when we want to fight, and humility when we desire praise.

Each day, we have a choice to live as a citizen of the kingdom of God and to make that our reality or to be a citizen of this world. Remember that God calls us to a higher standard and gives us the power of the Holy Spirit as citizens of his kingdom. And we know that Jesus reigns at the right hand of God.

Reflect

How can you act as a citizen of the kingdom of God today? What does that look like?

I praise you for redeeming me and forgiving my sins. Thank you for sending Jesus to transfer my soul to a life of freedom. Amen.

Capable

Moses said to God, "Who am I that I should go to Pharaoh and bring the Israelites out of Egypt?"

EXODUS 3:11 NIV

Moses found himself face-to-face with the Spirit of God in the form of a burning bush, and Moses wondered, *Who am I that I should be called?* Tradition tells us that Moses had a stutter, yet God still chose him to be his mouthpiece and lead God's people out of slavery. Moses believed in the power of God and knew that with God on his side, anything was possible, and no one could stop him. The same holds true for us today.

We are called to be the hands and feet of Jesus on this earth, and, of course, we will occasionally feel insecure, incapable, or underqualified. We may doubt our calling at times, but we still must obey God. And when we acknowledge him in all we do, we can have confidence that surpasses understanding.

Reflect

What do you want to try but also fear?
Take your first step in pursuing that today.

Thank you for calling me, Lord. I pray for courage and faith to pursue your purpose for me.

Saving Grace

It is by grace you have been saved, through faith—
and this is not from yourselves, it is the gift of God.

EPHESIANS 2:8 NIV

God is so good that his grace saved our souls, and that grace changes us for eternity. And when we fall in love with Jesus and experience his healing power, it shows. We are changed and different because we are made new. We don't act a certain way or do certain things to earn God's love, but we choose to pursue him out of our love for him.

Our past or our future can't separate us from the love of Jesus Christ. And the more time we spend in his Word, the more we want to be in his Word, yearning for his presence every day. We are called to be lights in this dark world. We are called to make a difference.

Reflect

Be different today by shining brightly and boldly for Jesus.

I thank you for the gift of your saving grace in my life.
You have loved and chosen me, and I praise your holy name,
Lord. Amen.

Discipline

Since we have these promises, dear friends, let us purify ourselves from everything that contaminates body and spirit, perfecting holiness out of reverence for God.

2 CORINTHIANS 7:1 NIV

It's said that the natural cycles in life are discovery, discipline, and delight. As a mom, I see this with my boys. My middle son has discovered his love for soccer, and as he has become more disciplined with practice, he has certainly improved. It is sheer delight when his practice pays off and he scores at game time. The same is true with our faith.

We discover God's Word and the joy of our faith, but we must remain disciplined so that we can experience the delight of God's presence. We aren't perfect, of course, but in Jesus we are being perfected, and we pursue holiness out of reverence for our Creator. Those of us who are actively grabbing hold of the promises of God's Word are advancing the kingdom. And what an honor and a privilege that is.

Reflect

In what area of your life do you need more discipline?

Lord, I want to pursue holiness and honor your name.
Purify my heart. Amen.

Surrender

"Abba, Father," he said, "everything is possible for you. Take this cup from me. Yet not what I will, but what you will."

MARK 14:36 NIV

"Not what I will, but what you will." Eight powerful words that illustrate total trust and surrender. God allows certain things to happen in our lives or wills them to happen, but either way, whatever our circumstance, we submit to the hand of God and rest in our trust in him. He has the power to control the universe, and we do not. And if God answered every prayer we prayed, it would be us sitting on the throne in heaven, not him.

Many of us struggle with the idea of submitting all to God, especially when it doesn't seem to make sense. What if we allowed God to rule our life? Whom we talk to, where we go, and how we spend our money? If we opened up our whole life to Jesus, would our lives look the same or different?

Reflect

With what present concern in your life can you tell the Lord, "Not my will but yours"?

Jesus, you know my prayers, wants, and needs. I submit. Not my will, Father, but yours. Amen.

Omnipresent

Where shall I go from your Spirit? Or where shall I flee from your presence? If I ascend to heaven, you are there! If I make my bed in Sheol, you are there!

PSALM 139:7–8 ESV

A few years ago, one of my best friends had leukemia, and she had to live in the hospital for over a month while she received treatment. I don't like the hospital, but my love language is quality time, and I made sure to visit her every chance I could get.

Driving to the hospital, I would cling to the promise of God's omnipresence, meaning he's anywhere and everywhere at all times. I knew he walked with me down the halls of the hospital and held my hand while I held hers. He gave me strength so that I could be the hands of Jesus to my bestie. And you know what? He *was* there. I have no doubt about it. There's no place we can go where Jesus isn't already there.

Reflect

Recall a time when you felt scared or far from God but still felt his presence. Praise him for that today.

Thank you for being with me right now, Lord.
Your presence gives me strength, joy, and peace.
I draw near to you, Father. Amen.

Fight for You

> "The LORD will fight for you,
> and you have only to be silent."
>
> EXODUS 14:14 ESV

Sometimes we will feel surrounded by our enemies, like the Israelites felt. Our enemy may be loneliness, addiction, doubt, pride—you can fill in the blank. The culprits may be different, but the feeling is the same: overwhelmed. In these moments, God whispers the same thing to us that he whispered to the Israelites, which is that we need only to be still and let the Lord fight for us.

Our weapons are our faith and our prayer. A melody of praise wrapped in our tears and desperation. I have lain on the floor, crying, not understanding God but trusting him. Submitting to his plan. My situation didn't change, but my heart did. Little by little, I saw the Red Sea in my life begin to part. Whatever it is, the Lord will work it out and fight for you.

Reflect

In what area of your life do you need to let God fight for you?

Lord, thank you for seeing me. I submit my worries to you, and I trust you. Amen.

Emotions

[The Lord] said to me, "You are my servant, Israel, in whom I will display my splendor." But I said, "I have labored in vain; I have spent my strength for nothing at all. Yet what is due me is in the LORD's hand, and my reward is with my God."

ISAIAH 49:3–4 NIV

God chose Isaiah to deliver a message of hope and deliverance to the Israelites. Isaiah also received a vision that was difficult for him to understand. Nevertheless, he had to make a critical yet difficult decision to trust God in the midst of bad news.

Isaiah had such strong faith because he trusted God not only with the situation but also with his emotions. He was honest with God and processed his pain and his feelings with the Lord. They had a real, honest relationship. Many times, we try to minimize our pain by hiding it when we should bring it to God, who will comfort and guide us through whatever raw emotions we're facing.

Reflect

Bring a pain, fear, doubt, or frustration to God today.

You are good, Lord, and you can handle all my emotions. I bring all of myself to you today. I thank you for your almighty name. I love you. Amen.

Difference-Maker

"What if they do not believe me or listen to me and say,
'The LORD did not appear to you'?" Then the LORD said to
[Moses], "What is that in your hand?" "A staff," he replied.

EXODUS 4:1–2 NIV

I love these verses because they reveal Moses' self-doubt and
humanity. God called him, but Moses still had questions and
fears. It goes to show that no one is above human emotions.
The difference with the difference-makers is that they push
the fear aside and obey. They walk and use what God has
given them to fulfill their calling.

The very thing that God used in Moses' life was already
at Moses' fingertips. I'm not sure what God has given you,
but perhaps the very thing that scares you might be exactly
what he made you for!

Reflect

Use what God has given you today to glorify him in a
tangible way, be it big or small.

*I thank you for your Holy Word, Lord. I thank you for the
stories and the men and women who inspire me and my own
faith. I pray that you will use me for your kingdom to serve as
a difference-maker. Amen.*

He Prepares Us

David left Gath and escaped to the cave of Adullam. When his brothers and his father's household heard about it, they went down to him there. All those who were in distress or in debt or discontented gathered around him, and he became their commander. About four hundred men were with him.

1 SAMUEL 22:1–2 NIV

When David was running from Saul and hiding in the cave of Adullam, God used that time to develop David's character and build his army. David didn't know the outcome of his situation, but he trusted God.

When we feel as though we're hiding in a cave or running for our life, we, too, can have faith that God has big plans for us. Although we may not know what's on the other side of any given moment, we know that God is in charge. Like he did with David, he can and will use that time to prepare us.

Reflect

What negative experience in your life has God used for his glory?

Lord, thank you for preparing me during hardships.
You are so good! Amen.

Confidence

Do not throw away your confidence;
it will be richly rewarded.

HEBREWS 10:35 NIV

I thought about this verse while driving my kids to school one day, and the "throw away" part of it stuck with me. "Throw Away." How do we throw away our confidence? By scrolling on Instagram, comparing ourselves to others, and listening to the negative voice inside our heads, to name a few.

The Bible specifically tells us to *not* throw away our confidence because it will be richly rewarded. Instead, we must guard it and remind ourselves of who we are in Christ and how he sees us. He has plans to give us a future full of hope. And when our confidence comes from a place of wholeness and health, we can lead others in being more confident as well. We can't give to others what we ourselves don't have.

Reflect

How do you personally "throw away" your confidence? Set new boundaries for yourself today that will help protect it.

My identity is rooted in you, Jesus. Help me find and safeguard my confidence so that I can help others find confidence in you too. Amen.

Little Things

> "Whoever can be trusted with very little can also be trusted with much, and whoever is dishonest with very little will also be dishonest with much."

LUKE 16:10 NIV

Our culture is obsessed with social media and its influencers, and as evangelist and author Christine Caine said, many people "want a blue check by their name but aren't as concerned with a heart check."[7] That is, people care more about being verified on social media platforms than they do about being influenced by the Holy Spirit. But God wants us to be bold and passionate about our calling, and that is precisely the kind of influencer we should want to be.

We will face opposition as believers. We will fail at times. If God can trust us with the little things, then he will trust us with the big things.

Reflect

Focus on the little moments today when God is calling you to a higher standard.

Lord, I pray that your Holy Spirit influences me so that I can boldly influence others, guiding them toward you. Amen.

---

7   Christine Caine, "Blue Check or Heart Check?," Facebook video, January 26, 2021.

Rejection

The entire town came out to meet Jesus,
but they begged him to go away and leave them alone.

MATTHEW 8:34 NLT

I often feel discouraged when I'm trying to be bold for Christ and people misunderstand or attack me. Then I remind myself that I am in good company! Jesus faced rejection when he preached about love. God called Noah to build an ark in a drought, and people laughed. The Lord summoned David to fight a giant with a slingshot, and no one believed in him. My pastor has said, "If God has put a Goliath in front of you, then he must know there's a David inside of you."

God calls up his church to preach his goodness and move in big ways in this world. We are his light, and we must be certain of that. Big, bold faith will lead to boldness in our life. I encourage you to build the ship in a drought if that's what you feel God is calling you to do. People might not understand, but those aren't your people.

Reflect

What is a calling on your life that you know you have? Don't be afraid to chase that dream. Take a step toward that calling today.

Lord, I accept your will over my life. I pray for favor and an anointing over my dreams. Amen.

Lydia

When she and the members of her household were baptized, she invited us to her home. "If you consider me a believer in the Lord," she said, "come and stay at my house." And she persuaded us.

ACTS 16:15 NIV

Today's verse tells of the conversion of Lydia, my namesake! I have pictured and studied this lady a lot over the years. I love that she identifies herself as a believer, invites people into her home, and then persuades them. Like Lydia, we are called to place our identity in Jesus. Not in our race, gender, job, home, marital status, kids, or appearance. None of those things holds our identity, even if the world tries to tell us otherwise. Our identity is only in the Lord.

Lydia was also hospitable, and we should be too. Ask someone to grab a coffee, have a lunch date, or go for a walk. The last thing we learn of Lydia in this verse is that she persuaded others. We, too, can be so firm in our faith and convictions that we draw others toward Jesus. That's how we can be difference-makers for Christ.

Reflect

Consider the three attributes of Lydia and pursue at least one of them today.

Lord, like Lydia, my identity is firmly planted in you. Help me to be hospitable and persuasive to others. Amen.

Omnipotent

To whom then will you compare me,
that I should be like him? says the Holy One.
Lift up your eyes on high and see: who created these? He
who brings out their host by number, calling them all by
name; by the greatness of his might and because he is strong
in power, not one is missing.

ISAIAH 40:25–26 ESV

Have you ever stopped to think about how powerful God is
to have created everything that we see, touch, and feel? The
same God who pursues us and knows the number of hairs
on our head made it all.

God is omnipotent, meaning all-powerful. He can
do anything! Praising him for his goodness doesn't make
him any better because he's self-existent and above our
understanding. Our self-obsessed world is put in its place
when we take the focus off ourselves and put it onto our
omnipotent Creator.

Reflect

Praise God today for his all-powerful nature.

Lord, you are mighty and powerful, and I praise your name.
Thank you for the beauty all around me that you created.
Amen.

Blameless

> "This God is my strong refuge
> and has made my way blameless."
>
> 2 SAMUEL 22:33 ESV

I want us to recognize two concepts from this verse today. The first is the idea that God is our "strong refuge." Let's break that down even smaller. God is ours, and he is strong, and he is a refuge. So what he offers us is a strong, safe place.

The second point is that his way is blameless. This may seem like a tall order, so I dug into Scripture. God describes several people in the Bible as blameless: Noah, Zechariah, and Job, to name just a few. Scripture notes that Noah drank too much wine (see Genesis 9:20–21) and describes Job as depressed (see Job 3:1), while Zechariah doubted God's promise to him (see Luke 1:13). Blameless doesn't mean perfection. We are saved because of Jesus, and it's okay if we mess up sometimes. We are still devoted to God, our refuge.

Reflect

Say this verse out loud today. Memorize it and
mark it on your heart.

*Lord, you are my safe place, and you are strong when I am
weak. You are mine, and I am yours. I love you. Amen.*

Never Forsake Us

Those who know your name trust in you, for you, LORD,
have never forsaken those who seek you.

PSALM 9:10 NIV

I have learned a lot about free will and the lies that the
Enemy uses to try to stop us from trusting Jesus. The devil
wants to convince us that our way is better than God's way.
It's almost as if we hear a whisper telling us that God is
somehow holding out on us, but that is a lie, my friend.

The Word of God promises that if we seek the Lord,
even when we don't know the "whys," God will come
through for us. We have to trust him even when things don't
seem to make sense. Sometimes things happen that we just
don't understand, but God's way is best. He is trustworthy
and will never forsake us.

Reflect

What is going on in your life that you don't understand but
are trying to trust God with? When doubt or fear creeps
into your mind today, take that thought captive and remind
yourself that you are choosing to trust him fully.

Thank you for being trustworthy, Father.
I know you will never forsake me. Amen.

Come Forth as Gold

"He knows the way that I take; when he has tested me,
I will come forth as gold."

JOB 23:10 NIV

Job is speaking about God in today's verse, and he said these words while facing major turmoil and uncertainty in his life. Although he was a blessed man, he lost everything. Despite his dire circumstances, he remained steadfast in his faith, certain that he would come forth as gold. What bold faith!

God does test us, and we all face uncertainty. Like Job, we must follow God's steps and trust that we, too, will come forth as gold. We can be confident in our faith when the going gets tough, and we can find comfort in knowing that it is part of God's plan for our life. He will walk us through any and every challenge that comes our way.

Reflect

How or when have you come forth as gold in your faith journey? Share that with a friend or loved one today.

Lord, I pray for confidence like Job's. I am thankful that you trust me and know the way that I will take. Amen.

Occupied with the Word

When Silas and Timothy arrived from Macedonia,
Paul was occupied with the word, testifying to the Jews
that the Christ was Jesus.

ACTS 18:5 ESV

This verse is so beautiful. It describes Paul as "occupied with the word." Other translations use the language "pressed in the spirit" (KJV) or "devoted himself exclusively" (NIV). Nevertheless, this verse shows how Paul was earnest and deeply enthralled with the Word of God.

It's also interesting to note that Paul testified once his friends arrived. It's true that there is a sense of comfort and boldness when your people rally with you. And perhaps Silas and Timothy handled other aspects so that Paul could "devote himself exclusively" to the Word. Everyone has a part to play in the kingdom of Christ.

Reflect

Testify to someone today that Jesus is Christ in your life.
You can share your testimony with another believer
but tell her what Jesus has done for you.

Jesus, you are the King of kings and Lord of lords. You are the ruler of heaven, and you take away the sins of the world. You are the way, the truth, and the life. Thank you for forgiving my transgressions so I am seen white as snow, pure, and holy. Amen.

He Looks at the Heart

The Lord said to Samuel, "Do not consider his appearance
or his height, for I have rejected him. The Lord does not
look at the things people look at. People look at the outward
appearance, but the Lord looks at the heart."

1 Samuel 16:7 niv

Historians agree that Jesus' physical appearance was nothing
exceptional, yet he is the Savior of the world. In the Old
Testament, David's own father overlooked him, but God had
big plans for David to become king and redeem God's people
to the Lord.

God doesn't judge by outward appearances; he sees
the heart. He sees our passions, our habits, our strengths,
and our weaknesses. He knows our thoughts and the things
that we focus our energy on. Yes, it is important to take
care of our bodies and be healthy, but physical appearance
is a concern of this world. We must remember that we are
spiritual beings first and foremost, and if God is concerned
with the things we can't see, then so should we be.

Reflect

Be aware of your thoughts today and avoid judging people.

*Thank you for knowing who I am
and my true self, Father. Amen.*

Made Alive

As by a man came death, by a man has come also the
resurrection of the dead. For as in Adam all die,
so also in Christ shall all be made alive.

1 CORINTHIANS 15:21–22 ESV

The Bible starts with Adam and ends with Jesus. It's a
beautiful story of redemption and God's pursuit of us. In
Christ, we are made alive, and this comes straight from the
Word of the Lord. We will rise from the dead, and our spirits
will be resurrected with Jesus. This is powerful, joyful news!

Depression, anxiety, loneliness, and dissatisfaction
haunt so many of us. Perhaps that's you today. Or maybe
you're distracted by to-do lists or caught up in the daily
grind of life. We can find peace in knowing that the truth
remains the same: Jesus Christ gives eternal life to all who
believe in him. May I gently remind you that we know who
wins in the end. We know how the story goes and have read
the last page of the book. We are on the side of the hero, and
the hero loves us.

Reflect

Do you fear death? If so, take that to Jesus today.

*Lord, thank you for pursuing me
and for sending your Son, Jesus. Amen.*

Overcome the World

"I have told you these things, so that in me you may have peace. In this world you will have trouble. But take heart! I have overcome the world."

JOHN 16:33 NIV

Despite our current cancel culture, the truth of God is black and white. And the more we try to fit in or avoid rocking the boat, the greater we risk losing our peace. If we aren't standing up for Jesus, then we're giving in to the world around us. We are mistaking the peace that God offers, the peace that surpasses our understanding, for a counterfeit peace that the world attempts to sell us.

Remember that we are called to be in this world but not of this world. Jesus is the Prince of Peace. We have peace because of the promises found in God's Word. Our situations may be anything but peaceful, yet we overflow with peace because our focus is on eternal things. Jesus overcame the world, and his Holy Spirit lives inside of us. There is no greater peace, sweet friend!

Reflect

In what area are you fighting with God? Today, promise him and yourself that you will have peace over the situation.

You have overcome the world, Jesus!
I place my trust in you. Amen.

Intended for Good

Even though you intended to hurt me, God intended it for good. It was his plan all along, to ensure the survival of many people.

GENESIS 50:20 TPT

Joseph spoke these words. His brothers had sold him into slavery, and he had every reason to harbor anger and bitterness. By human standards, his unforgiveness would have been justified, yet we read how Joseph truly forgave his brothers in his soul. He didn't let his circumstances define him. His path seemed hopeless at times, but he was confident in the Lord, knowing God would use everything for good. What a shining example of trusting God.

Let's go back to the first part of the verse: "Even though you intended to hurt me, God intended it for good." Let that beautiful truth cover you today. Whatever storm you find yourself in right now, trust that God will use it for good. As we surrender to Jesus, he will use our story to testify to his goodness.

Reflect

Recall a time when someone or something intended to hurt you, but God used it for good. Praise him for that today.

Lord, thank you for using all things in my life for good. Even when I feel helpless and my circumstances are unfair, you reign. You still make all things for your glory. Amen.

His Holy Name

Praise the LORD, my soul;
all my inmost being, praise his holy name.

PSALM 103:1 NIV

Praise is the response of a grateful heart, and we praise the Lord because we yearn for his presence. We draw near to him because we love him, and our praise is our response to that love. He doesn't need our praise, but he deserves it.

When we approach the Lord with praise, the atmosphere shifts. It becomes difficult to complain, harbor bitterness, or carry anger when we focus our inmost being on praising the King of kings for his goodness and holy nature. While we are in his presence, we feel the peace that surpasses understanding, and we develop courage. Many people even tear up when they praise Jesus because the power of God's Spirit is so overwhelming that our bodies feel it deeply.

Reflect

Praise God today and meditate on his holy name.

Lord, I praise your holy name. You are powerful, loving, mighty, and good. I worship you. Amen.

Completion

I am sure of this, that he who began a good work in you will
bring it to completion at the day of Jesus Christ.

PHILIPPIANS 1:6 ESV

Many of us replay the pains of yesterday instead of
celebrating the promises of tomorrow. Yes, things have
happened in our lives, and we all have experienced pain and
hurt, but God is powerful. When the devil reminds us of our
past, we show him the promises of our future. God has big
plans to use us for his glory. He will use our story for good
no matter how dark it may be.

Because we are rooted in Jesus, our confidence rests in
the Lord. When we have confidence, we often experience
calmness. I don't know about you, but my mind can be
turbulent with anxious thoughts, counting all the reasons
why I should be stressed out. Yet today's verse reminds us
that we have every reason to enjoy confidence and calmness
about our future.

Reflect

Think of three goals you have for next month.
Have confidence in them.

*Thank you for knowing me, Lord. You know my past
and my future, and I trust you with my life. Amen.*

Anxious about Nothing

Do not be anxious about anything, but in every situation,
by prayer and petition, with thanksgiving,
present your requests to God.

PHILIPPIANS 4:6 NIV

Is it truly possible for us to live our lives anxious about nothing? How can we be expected to pray in every situation? As our verse today reveals, the key to having peace in all situations is to live a life of prayer.

This doesn't mean moving around on our knees or becoming a monk. We can, however, train our minds to be aware of God's presence at all times. Knowing that God is always with us, that he loves us, and that he is in control gives us a sense of peace that transcends understanding. But note how the verse instructs us to also come with thanksgiving. We are blessed to have a Father to cast our anxieties to, and he is worthy of our praise.

Reflect

Memorize this verse today so that your heart is prepared the next time you begin to feel anxious.

I am so thankful for who you are and all you have done in my life, Lord. All my fears and worries I lay at your feet. I know you are faithful and in control. I trust you. Amen.

Intercede

In the same way, the Spirit helps us in our weakness. We do
not know what we ought to pray for, but the Spirit himself
intercedes for us through wordless groans. And he who
searches our hearts knows the mind of the Spirit,
because the Spirit intercedes for God's people
in accordance with the will of God.

ROMANS 8:26–27 NIV

Are you afraid to pray aloud in a group setting? Or perhaps
you are so overwhelmed with life sometimes that you don't
even know how to begin to pray. Our verse today is good
news that brings power and comfort. What a promise it is to
know that the Spirit himself intercedes for us, giving us the
words to pray.

Jesus is so in love and in tune with us that he sends his
Spirit to intercede and intervene on our behalf, pleading for
our needs, according to his will. When we don't know what
to say, the Lord guides us.

Reflect

During your prayer time today, allow the Holy Spirit of God
to speak through you.

*I praise you for the power of the Holy Spirit, Lord.
Thank you for knowing me and loving me. Amen.*

June

Our Helper

We can say with confidence,
"The LORD is my helper, so I will have no fear.
What can mere people do to me?"

HEBREWS 13:6 NLT

It's easy to let fear get in our own way. We fear rejection, failure, or the unknown. We can even make decisions out of fear. Our verse today reminds us not to be afraid. God is love, and love drives out fear.

Can you say with confidence that the Lord is your helper? Another way to think of a helper is as a coworker. In other words, God is our helper, working with us on this journey of life. We don't have to fear anything that today might bring because we know that we walk with Jesus. Not only is God the King of the physical world, but he is also the King of the spiritual world that's all around us. We could not be in better, safer hands.

Reflect

Make every decision today based on the truth
that God is your helper.

Father, you are my helper, and that truth overwhelms me with gratitude. I am yours, and I praise you for your holy name. Amen.

Grace of God

"I do not set aside the grace of God, for if righteousness could be gained through the law, Christ died for nothing!"

Galatians 2:21 niv

Before we dive into the verse for today, let's review a little bit about the words that appear. The Hebrew word for "grace" is *channan*, or *charis* in Greek, meaning "the state of kindness and favor toward someone, often with a focus on a benefit given to the object."[8]

What Paul is saying is that, of course, we remember God's grace, or his kind favor, toward us. But that doesn't mean that we don't also pursue our relationship with him. His grace actually fuels our love to grow even deeper. And because of his love, we gladly hand over our lives to him and still continue our pursuit of him. We can't do anything to earn more of his love, but we can enjoy freedom in the grace found in Jesus.

Reflect

Consider the ways in which you invest in
your relationship with God. Are these out of obligation
or love for your Master?

Lord, I desire more of you. Thank you for pouring your love and grace all over my life. Amen.

8   Strong, *Strong's Expanded Exhaustive Concordance of the Bible*, #548.

Straight Paths

Trust in the LORD with all your heart, and do not lean on your own understanding. In all your ways acknowledge him, and he will make straight your paths.

PROVERBS 3:5–6 ESV

I love the English Standard Version translation of this verse, particularly, "He will make straight your paths." This promise is so powerful. I often don't feel as though I'm on a straight path. I feel like I swerve this way and that and, some days, without any clear direction.

We can be assured that no matter our circumstances or past decisions, God will make straight our paths. How? Faith. We are called to have faith. Even when our understanding of the workings of the world falls short or we're unclear as to what steps we need to take to succeed, we trust our maker. We listen to him. We ask him to govern our life, and we trust him with all our heart.

Reflect

What path in your life does not feel straight right now? It could be your work life, home life, or something else. Whatever it is, pray over it today.

Make straight my paths, Lord. You are good and trustworthy. Amen.

Yoked

Do not be yoked together with unbelievers. For what do righteousness and wickedness have in common? Or what fellowship can light have with darkness? What harmony is there between Christ and Belial? Or what does a believer have in common with an unbeliever? What agreement is there between the temple of God and idols? For we are the temple of the living God.

2 CORINTHIANS 6:14–16 NIV

To yoke yourself together means to join or combine, and as today's verse explains, it helps to yoke together with fellow believers. Life can be hard, and some days I come home exhausted. Nothing drastic necessarily happened, but I walk in the door feeling a little bit like I've returned from battle.

But seeing my husband's face brings a sense of relief because we're on the same team. We are yoked as believers, so there is harmony and agreement between us. The same is true with my close friends. I choose my inner circle carefully so that it's full of believers whose faith inspires mine.

Reflect

Who are you yoked with? Are you equally yoked?
Pray for him today.

Lord, I praise you for your Word and your wisdom. Thank you for the people you have placed in my life. Amen.

Righteous

The LORD is far from the wicked,
but he hears the prayers of the righteous.

PROVERBS 15:29 NLT

The Bible features dozens of anointed men and women whom God considered righteous even though their actions sometimes fell short of expectation. And you know what they all shared in common? Steadfast faith.

Whenever we feel as though we're falling short, we must remember that because of our faith, we are also considered righteous. And as today's verse assures us, God hears our prayers. Do you personally know a prayer warrior whose prayer time seems extra anointed? It's as if when they pray, their words hold more power and carry more weight. I want that kind of prayer life, and I want to be that kind of friend to others. We, too, can become anointed prayer warriors.

Reflect

Remind yourself throughout the day of your righteousness in faith. Let that truth embolden your prayers.

Thank you for hearing my prayers, Lord. Help me become a prayer warrior whose steadfast faith inspires others. Amen.

Faith

Faith is confidence in what we hope for and assurance about what we do not see. This is what the ancients were commended for.

HEBREWS 11:1–2 NIV

I love that Hebrews gives us a clear definition of faith. Let's read it a second time: "Faith is confidence in what we hope for and assurance about what we do not see." Then, a few verses later in Hebrews, we read that it is impossible to please God without our faith (see 11:6). Clearly our faith is important, and so many truths rest on it, so it's important for us to understand what that means and looks like in our lives.

First, our faith cracks open the freedom and promises that God offers us. Second, we learned that we are considered righteous if we have faith. And as today's verse tells us, the ancients received praise for their faith. If we want to please and honor God, then we must be rooted in him so that we trust his will and place our hope in whatever he has in store for us.

Reflect

Memorize the definition of faith found in Hebrews 11:1.

Lord, thank you for my faith. I love you, and it is my heart's desire to grow deeper in love with you, expressed through my faith. I invite you into my every moment today. Amen.

Patiently Waiting

In this hope we were saved. Now hope that is seen is not hope. For who hopes for what he sees? But if we hope for what we do not see, we wait for it with patience.

ROMANS 8:24–25 ESV

In these verses from Romans, Paul is talking about the hope we have in our future glory, when we are resurrected and united with God as his children. We know that this gift is certain, but we can't see it because we are not home yet, so we must wait patiently in hope.

Is it hard for you to step out in faith? I find myself acting in bad faith sometimes, expecting God to show up right away, even though I know that's not necessarily how he works. It's this beautiful balance of expecting and waiting. As concepts, expecting and waiting seem to be opposites, but in the life of a Christian, they actually go hand in hand.

Reflect

What are you hoping for from God today? I challenge you to tell someone. There is power and accountability when we speak our faith into action.

Lord, thank you for saving me. My hope is in you, Jesus. You are King, and I wait patiently, trusting your will. Amen.

He Strengthens Us

I can do all things through him who strengthens me.

PHILIPPIANS 4:13 ESV

Paul wrote this verse while he was in prison, probably at Rome or Ephesus. Sitting in his jail cell, he was still full of hope, faith, and confidence. Nothing could separate him from the truth and power he found in the Holy Spirit. The same power, faith, and hope that Paul held on to is offered to us.

We tend to allow the lies of our culture or the darkness of our circumstances to dim the light of Jesus. But today let's focus on God's power in our very midst. Our doubts or circumstances do not change or affect him. He is the same yesterday as he is today: good, loving, and rich in mercy. He knows us, he loves us, and he's rooting for us. We can do anything that lies before us today because of him who strengthens us.

Reflect

When you feel challenged, worried, or weak today, repeat Philippians 4:13 to yourself as many times as you need to.

I am a conqueror, Lord, and I pray that you continue to transform my perspective to see the world as you do. Give me the heart for your people. Help me love. In Jesus' name, amen.

Prayer

"The eyes of the Lord are on the righteous and his ears are attentive to their prayer, but the face of the Lord is against those who do evil."

1 PETER 3:12 NIV

The idea that God is attentive to my words during prayer honestly floors me even though today's verse reminds me that it shouldn't. He isn't distracted or bored with our prayers; he wants us to talk to him, and he's listening. Praying is the greatest thing a believer can do. It connects us to our Creator, and it's our lifeline to Jesus.

We want to have our own God stories and that can only happen through a relationship with Jesus. In fact, we should talk to God more than we talk to anyone else. I wouldn't expect to be close with my husband or best friend if I never talked to them. God wants the best for us; we just need to make our hearts available to him. Miracles await our prayers!

Reflect

Spend more time than usual in prayer today. Be intentional and seek Jesus. Open your heart up to him, knowing he's listening attentively to you.

Thank you for listening attentively to my prayers, Lord.
I seek and worship you, Father. Amen.

Fear the Lord

Be not wise in your own eyes;
fear the LORD, and turn away from evil.

PROVERBS 3:7 ESV

Growing up, when I used to hear the expression, "fear the Lord," I thought it meant to literally be afraid of God. When I grew older, I understood that to "fear the Lord" means and encompasses so much more. It means having reverence for God, trusting him, and heeding his wisdom. To fear the Lord is to honor his Word and hold him in the highest esteem.

Additionally, we must shun evil. *To shun* has connotations of abhorrence and loathing. This is the proper response to anything impure or morally filthy, but in our culture, moral corruption seems to be celebrated and used to market products. We must cling to God's truth and fear the Lord now more than ever.

Reflect

In what ways do you tend to be "wise in your own eyes"? Be mindful of that today, remembering to prioritize God's wisdom above all else.

Jesus, thank you for your Word, wisdom, and pure Spirit. Amen.

Move Mountains

"You don't have enough faith," Jesus told them. "I tell you the truth, if you had faith even as small as a mustard seed, you could say to this mountain, 'Move from here to there,' and it would move. Nothing would be impossible."

MATTHEW 17:20 NLT

The Bible is full of encouragement to have faith and to demonstrate it through our words and deeds. Faith isn't belief without truth; it's pursuing the truth and acting boldly, even when we can't see the next step. Faith is trust without reservation, and it's required if we want to mature in our relationship with Jesus.

Jesus promises us that anything is possible with faith, even if that faith is as small as a seed. What a beautiful image and powerful message. Even though the seed is planted under a lot of dirt and weight, it isn't crushed. It cracks open and grows into something beautiful, created by God. Let's remember that we can move mountains with our faith.

Reflect

How big is your faith? Imagine yourself as a seed, growing more in your faith every day. If you're lacking faith over something in your life, talk to God about it today.

Lord, thank you for pursuing me. Thank you for always being enough for me. My hope is in you. Amen.

Unaware

They were kept from recognizing him.
LUKE 24:16 NIV

Sometimes we are unaware of God's presence. We may feel like everything around us is going poorly or wrong, and that may be the case, but God remains in control. That's why we must not rely on our emotions but our knowledge in our one true God.

Today we live a harvest of yesterday's thoughts. Our thoughts become words, and our words become actions. Just because we can't see God moving in our midst doesn't mean that he isn't up to something wonderful. We believe that his promises are true and that his character is unchanging. We must have faith in him even when we might not understand his will.

Reflect

What does today reveal about your thoughts from yesterday? How can you choose healthy habits today to reap a beautiful harvest tomorrow?

Lord, I know that you are God. You are the same yesterday, today, and tomorrow. Your greatness is not based on my circumstances or emotions. Thank you for always being a mighty God. Amen.

Love, Love, Love

[Love] always protects, always trusts, always hopes, always perseveres. Love never fails. But where there are prophecies, they will cease; where there are tongues, they will be stilled; where there is knowledge, it will pass away.

1 CORINTHIANS 13:7–8 NIV

The Bible tells us that love comes from God, who is love. The word *love* in our text today was translated from the Greek word *agape*. This type of love is always demonstrative, meaning it's not a feeling but an action. In fact, God calls us to love whether we feel like it or not, whether we feel the other person has earned it or not, and even when it's a sacrifice.

There is so much for us to learn about love. Are you feeling unloved? Are you waiting for love? Finding it hard to love? Notice how powerful love can be. It heals us, gives us hope, and never fails. Everyone will know we belong to Jesus when we lead with love.

Reflect

Show love, be love, and act in love today.

Lord, thank you for your eternal love. Amen.

Faith from Hearing

Faith comes from hearing the message, and the message is heard through the word about Christ.

ROMANS 10:17 NIV

We're often too scared to pray big prayers or take big risks out of fear of failure. We wonder how we could still trust God after failure. How would we recover? When we think and act like this, we don't invite God's greatness to show up for us. We have baby faith instead of great big faith.

What makes today's verse so powerful is that Paul gives us the secret to increasing our faith: hearing God's Word. Our faith in Jesus grows as we read and spend time in his Word, sing his Word, and talk about his Word. We can't expect big things from little faith. Faith comes from hearing the message of Jesus.

Reflect

Read God's Word today to grow your faith.

Thank you for giving me all the resources I need to flourish, Lord. I want my faith to move mountains. I want my life to inspire those around me to seek your glory. Use me for your kingdom, Lord. Increase my faith. Amen.

Contentment

I have learned to be content whatever the circumstances. I know what it is to be in need, and I know what it is to have plenty. I have learned the secret of being content in any and every situation, whether well fed or hungry, whether living in plenty or in want. I can do all this through him who gives me strength.

PHILIPPIANS 4:11–13 NIV

What could be better than contentment? In our Scripture passage today, Paul is telling the Philippians that he has learned the secret to contentment. Do you see it tucked away in verse 13?

Notice how Paul uses the word *learned*. He wasn't given contentment. He did not reach contentment. He says he learned how to be content. A second interesting thing we see is that he learned how to be content by trusting Jesus. Paul knows that he can conquer anything that's thrown at him because he lives in the knowledge that Jesus is in control.

Reflect

I challenge you today to try to learn contentment by resting in the knowledge that you, like Paul, can handle whatever life throws your way with the help of Jesus Christ.

Lord, thank you for this beautiful day. I pray that I will rest in your strength, Lord. Amen.

Break the Chains

Am I now trying to win the approval of human beings, or of God? Or am I trying to please people? If I were still trying to please people, I would not be a servant of Christ.

GALATIANS 1:10 NIV

We could post Galatians 1:10 to our Instagram and believe its truth with our whole heart only to find ourselves, a few hours later, checking the number of likes the post received. What is inside of us that seeks this approval?

Understanding and knowing with our entire being that Jesus is all we need to live a full life breaks the chains of people-pleasing and ushers in a life of joy. Paul connects breaking the chains of people-pleasing to serving Christ. We have to decide if we want to serve Jesus or the opinions of others. Once we make the decision of whom we will serve, we must continue to make that decision in our life day by day, moment by moment.

Reflect

Identify whom you are trying to please in your life.
Our awareness of unhealthy habits is the first step
to creating new, healthy ones.

Lord, I desire to be your servant. I want to serve you.
Please be the focus of my heart's desires and help me
in areas where I am insecure. Amen.

Only Son

"God so loved the world, that he gave his only Son,
that whoever believes in him should not perish
but have eternal life."

JOHN 3:16 ESV

Today's verse is perhaps the most famous verse in the whole Bible. It's often the first verse that kids memorize at Sunday school, and I even have memories of people holding cardboard signs displaying John 3:16 at sporting events. This verse is important because it demonstrates God's love for us; he gave up his only Son to save all of humanity.

John 3:16 assures us that our belief in Jesus will give us eternal life. Jesus not only frees us from death after life but also frees us of the chains we carry today. Love drives out fear, surpassing those fears of the unknown and death, and our familiarity with the verse should not take away or minimize the power of these words. We live in freedom because of our faith in Jesus Christ.

Reflect

What chains are you carrying today?
Talk to God about releasing them to him today.

*I praise you, Father, for sending Jesus. All glory to you.
I love you. Amen.*

Taste and See

I sought the LORD, and he answered me and delivered me from all my fears. Those who look to him are radiant, and their faces shall never be ashamed…Oh, taste and see that the LORD is good! Blessed is the man who takes refuge in him!

PSALMS 34:4–5, 8 ESV

David wrote most of the Psalms, and in a few verses before these, he wrote that there is no reason to fear. And I love how, after David prayed, God not only answered his prayers but also calmed David's fears. That's why the Psalms reiterate that there's no need to be fearful.

Sometimes we know things to be true deep in our hearts, but our feelings take over and convince us otherwise. We let our heads or our circumstances challenge the truth that is planted in our souls. As David tells us, we can taste and see that the Lord is good. We are blessed for our faith in him, friend!

Reflect

Live today in faith, not fear. Be mindful of your thoughts, and any time fear threatens to enter your heart, declare over yourself that the Lord is good and draw close to him.

Lord, I know that you are good.
I find refuge in you, Jesus. Amen.

Wherever You Go

"Have I not commanded you? Be strong and courageous.
Do not be frightened, and do not be dismayed, for the LORD
your God is with you wherever you go."

JOSHUA 1:9 ESV

I love the context of this verse. Moses had died, and Joshua
had become the new leader, preparing to lead the Israelites
into their promised land. This is the third time that the Lord
tells Joshua to be strong and courageous, but this time he
adds a reason: "for the LORD your God is with you wherever
you go."

The reason we have strength and courage is because
we know that God is with us no matter what. Our strength
and courage are not based on our own talents, feelings, or
circumstances. And our boldness and grit aren't based on
our wisdom or personality. Our strength and courage come
from our faith in the Lord on high.

Reflect

Be mindful of God's presence today. He is with you,
so let this reality make you bolder. Finally, tell a close friend
about the bold steps you plan to take, and ask her
to hold you accountable.

I am not frightened, for I know you are always with me, Lord.
Thank you for giving me your Spirit of power. Amen.

In Your Heart

Jesus knew what they were thinking and asked,
"Why are you thinking these things in your hearts?"

LUKE 5:22 NIV

Have you ever thought something in your heart but didn't have the courage to say it out loud? In today's verse, without the Pharisees and teachers of the law saying a word to Jesus, Jesus knew that they doubted his authority to forgive the sins of others. He knows the things in our hearts, and to be known is a beautiful gift. Jesus offers us this gift through a relationship with him. He loves, pursues, and adores us. We cannot hide from him anywhere.

Although the verse refers to the negative thoughts of the Pharisees and teachers, we can apply the same question to our dreams. Do you carry a dream, desire, or ambition in your heart that you're scared to pursue? God didn't put desires in us to tease us or taunt us. He wants you to pursue that dream. He knows that your dreams are inside of you, and he wants you to crack them open.

Reflect

Picture Jesus hearing your every thought today.
Be mindful and accountable.

Thank you for seeing me and knowing my innermost places. I want to know you more, Lord. Please continue to reveal yourself to me. Amen.

Pure in Heart

Blessed are the pure in heart,
for they will see God.

MATTHEW 5:8 NIV

What does "pure of heart" mean? Our hearts are pure when we seek the Lord for the pureness of his presence, not for favor, status, or monetary gain. We seek him out of a pure faith, for he is the great I AM, and his presence alone satisfies us. Our hearts desire God because of who he is, not what he can do for us.

We want to see God. We want to see his fingerprints throughout our day—his glory, faithfulness, love, compassion, and kindness. In our verse today, Jesus is telling his disciples that all of that is possible. The pure in heart *will* see God.

Reflect

Have you spent time with the Lord just to spend time with the Lord? Sit in his presence today.

Lord, I praise you for making yourself available to me.
I long for you. I pursue you. I choose you.
Thank you for loving me. Amen.

God Is Greater

Whenever our heart condemns us,
God is greater than our heart,
and he knows everything.

1 JOHN 3:20 ESV

I spent time wrestling with the idea that our own hearts condemn us, but it's true. Even when we try to take a step of faith in boldness, our own hearts question us, and our thoughts put us down. We are constantly telling ourselves lies, but we can take control of those lies and stop listening to them. Our hearts condemn us, but God is greater than our hearts.

God speaks answers to us. He speaks truth and wisdom. And we are called to know God's truth and to believe it. Let's stop listening to our heart's condemnation and accusations of unworthiness and go to battle with the truth. We belong, and we are beautifully and wonderfully made!

Reflect

Be mindful of when your heart is condemning you today.
Stand up against it and declare God's truth.

You know everything, Lord. Thank you for being greater than my heart. Continue to pour your Spirit into me. Amen.

Run with Endurance

Since we are surrounded by so great a cloud of witnesses,
let us also lay aside every weight, and sin which clings so
closely, and let us run with endurance the race that
is set before us.

HEBREWS 12:1 ESV

As believers, we should have a confidence complex. We should know where our identity lies and who God created us to be, and we should walk in freedom with determination and passion. When we are fixed on Jesus and our gaze is solely on him, we are unstoppable.

Of course, there will be moments of doubt, fear, and sorrow. Yet today's verse reminds us that we are surrounded by believers cheering us on as we run our own personal races. We are united with the legacy of God's family. You've got this, girl!

Reflect

What are you pursuing in life right now?
Is this what Jesus has set before you?

Lord, thank you for the people you have placed in my life to cheer me on. I pray I would be someone who cheers on others. Amen.

Builders

Wise people are builders—they build families, businesses, communities. And through intelligence and insight their enterprises are established and endure. Because of their skilled leadership, the hearts of people are filled with the treasures of wisdom and the pleasures of spiritual wealth. Wisdom can make anyone into a mighty warrior, and revelation-knowledge increases strength.

PROVERBS 24:3–5 TPT

You are a builder, sweet sister! You are a wise woman, and God is calling you to build. What a beautiful purpose. This promise reminds us that we are filled with wisdom, and with that wisdom comes strength.

I'm not sure what you are going through right now, but you have the strength to make it through this battle. You have the wisdom to build something beautiful. Be bold and stay your course!

Reflect

What are you building right now?
Spend time praying over that.

Thank you for giving me wisdom that is spiritual wealth. I am rich in you, Jesus! What an honor and privilege. I love you, Lord, and I am your vessel to use in big and mighty ways. Amen.

Fan into Flame

For this reason I remind you to fan into flame the gift of
God, which is in you through the laying on of my hands.

2 TIMOTHY 1:6 NIV

Picture a campfire and the flames slowly going out. On the
ground are embers still burning. If you fan or blow slowly
on the embers, the oxygen makes them hot again. Throw
some paper and logs on the embers, and you'll have yourself
a campfire again. That is what Paul means when he says "fan
into flame" the gift of God.

When we have an encounter with Jesus, we must
continue to fan the flames of our faith, our gift from God.
We must be intentional and honor the Lord and the gifts he
has given us.

Reflect

Fan the flames of your faith today, however that looks to you.

*Lord, I thank you for my faith. Help me in my unbelief and
any areas in which I have relied on myself or become stale.
I want to be all in for you, Jesus. Amen.*

At God's Command

By faith we understand that the universe was formed at
God's command, so that what is seen was not
made out of what was visible.

HEBREWS 11:3 NIV

The whole universe was formed at God's command. I
feel like we need to stop right there and take that in for a
moment. The whole universe was formed because God said
so! What we see today God made of things that weren't seen.
And by faith we are called to understand that.

It reminds me of the phrase "behind the scenes," and
God is always working behind the scenes. The Lord doesn't
operate on our level. How egotistical and closed-minded it
would be to think that God works on the same playing field
as we do. Today's verse really puts us in our place.

Reflect

Spend some time in nature today and worship the Lord
for all his creation.

*Jesus, thank you for speaking the universe into creation. You
are so big and mighty, and I worship your holy name. Amen.*

Shielded and Protected

Through your faith, God is protecting you by his power until
you receive this salvation, which is ready to be revealed on
the last day for all to see.

1 PETER 1:5 NLT

The Greek term used in this verse is *phroureo*, a military
term, also translated to mean "to guard" or "to keep."[9] It is
not through the power of our faith that we are protected. It is
through the power of God.

This verse isn't saying that we will be protected from
suffering. We know that we live in this world and are not yet
in heaven. Heartache and pain, both emotional and physical,
are part of our life on earth. But God's power, which protects
us until the end times, shields us. Do you feel that truth in
your life? It is a reality we must claim and take hold of.

Reflect

Be mindful today of God's power keeping and protecting you.

*Lord, thank you for protecting me in ways I am not even
aware of. I lean into you and your power. Amen.*

---

9   From *Strong's Concordance*, #5432, "phroureo," as cited on
     biblehub.com.

Lioness

The people rise like a lioness;
they rouse themselves like a lion.

NUMBERS 23:24 NIV

Lionesses are amazing creatures. They are powerful and smart. Fierce and mystical. Rise like the lioness that God created you to be. Whatever your gift is, make room for it. Pour time and effort into the passion or gift that God has given you.

God will always watch what you do in secret before he gives you a platform in the public space. Sometimes we want to be women of influence, but God can't trust us with the little things. Show yourself that you truly are a lioness.

Reflect

Rise up today! What brought you to this season won't take you to the next. What do you need to do in this season to level up to the next?

Jesus, you are mighty and have given me your powerful Holy Spirit. I pray I would rise up in your name for your glory, Lord. Amen.

Every Single Moment

Every single moment you are thinking of me!
How precious and wonderful to consider that you
cherish me constantly in your every thought!
PSALM 139:17–18 TPT

David is talking about God's love for him in this verse, and we are loved just the same. Our maker adores and cherishes us, and no one can take that away from us. Our own dark deeds, words, or thoughts can't even take it away from us. God knows us and can't stop thinking about us.

We break free when we realize how much Jesus cherishes us. We are called to live in hope. We journey from glory to glory, and our lives are destined to be a glorious adventure, not a struggle of hardship. Yes, we will have turmoil, but in every single moment, God is thinking about us.

Reflect

Meditate on the truth that God cherishes you all the time.
Let that change the way you go about your day today.

Lord, I am overwhelmed by your love for me. Thank you for loving me so well. I desire to receive your love, Lord. Amen.

Something New

I am about to do something new. See, I have already begun!
Do you not see it? I will make a pathway through the
wilderness. I will create rivers in the dry wasteland.

ISAIAH 43:19 NLT

Every year, my boys' school chooses a verse for all the kids to memorize. One year, Isaiah 43:19 was the chosen verse, and to hear my little seven-year-old repeat and memorize these words touched my heart. The power and faith of his pure heart, proclaiming this fresh and hopeful promise was never lost on me. I cherish that memory to this day.

This verse offers a beautiful promise that God is doing something new in each of us. He can make a way through the wilderness. He will create rivers out of dry wastelands. Do you see it? It is okay, sweet friend, if you can't see it yet. Trust that he is at work all around us, and, in fact, he has already begun.

Reflect

Read this verse aloud with conviction and childlike faith.

*Thank you for beginning something new in me, Jesus.
Give me eyes to see you moving in my life. Amen.*

July

Hold Fast

Let us hold fast the confession of our hope without wavering,
for He who promised is faithful.

HEBREWS 10:23 NKJV

I also love the New Living Translation of this same verse.
It reads, "Let us hold tightly without wavering to the hope
we affirm, for God can be trusted to keep his promise." Let's
break this verse down together.

Paul writes to encourage us, as believers, to hold fast,
or hold tightly to our hope. What does that look like? To
me, it means to focus on hope, not on our problems. To rest
in the Lord's presence. To hold tightly to our hope in Jesus
is to know his Word and to study it. Our faith increases as
we spend time in the Word of God. The last part of Paul's
encouragement is that God is faithful. Do you believe and
act according to the belief that God is faithful?

Reflect

Spend time with God recalling times when he has been
faithful in your life in the past.

*You are so faithful to me, Lord. I hold tightly to
the hope that is you, Jesus. Amen.*

Demolish Strongholds

The weapons we fight with are not the weapons of the world. On the contrary, they have divine power to demolish strongholds.

2 CORINTHIANS 10:4 NIV

Our verse today is such a beautiful reminder that we are not of this world. The rules of this world are not what we serve. Our citizenship is in heaven. When someone wrongs us, we don't fight back with gossip or slander. We don't use the weapons of this world. We use divine power from Jesus. We choose a healthy response because we are healthy women of the Lord.

When we have a worldly stronghold in our life, we need to have divine power to demolish it. We don't attack that grip on us with the tools of this world but with the supernatural help of the Holy Spirit.

Reflect

Be mindful today of any strongholds you may have in your life. Talk to Jesus about them.

Lord, I praise you for being God and for pouring your divine power over me. Thank you, Lord. Amen.

Rest

Truly my soul finds rest in God;
my salvation comes from him.

PSALM 62:1 NIV

Is your soul at rest today? Does your soul need rest? We can find rest in God. Nothing gives us peace like the presence of our Lord. When our soul truly surrenders to God's plan for our life, the truth that he is working everything out for his good not only comforts us but also empowers us to take bold steps of faith.

God hasn't given you passions or dreams to cause you distress or to confuse you. He wants to come alongside us to give us the desires of our hearts and, ultimately, our salvation. When our hearts align with the Lord's will and we walk with him in a real, intimate way, we find rest in him.

Reflect

Think of your dreams and passions. Do you have rest in your soul with what God is calling you to step into?

You are a good God. I know you place desires in my heart because you want me to pursue my dreams. I trust you, God. My soul finds rest in your promises. Amen.

Trust

Jesus replied, "You do not realize now what I am doing,
but later you will understand."

JOHN 13:7 NIV

God is always interested in our hearts. He desires us to seek
him, choose him, and trust him. I once heard someone
say that TRUST stands for Totally Relying Upon Superior
Timing. Do you trust the Lord with the timing of your life?
Jesus knows we won't understand what he's doing or why he
is doing it, but he promises us that later we will understand.

Looking back on my life, I see why God answered some
prayers with a no. I can see why he closed some doors. I still
don't understand certain things, but I trust God, and I know
that later I will understand. Part of trusting God is trusting
his timing. He created time, and he created us, so it's safe to
say that his plan is better than ours.

Reflect

Be mindful today to trust God with the timing of your life.

*Lord, I don't understand or even realize all that you are doing
in my midst, but I trust you. I surrender to your will,
your way, and your timing. Amen.*

The Lord's Purpose

Many are the plans in a person's heart,
but it is the LORD's purpose that prevails.

PROVERBS 19:21 NIV

I don't know about you, but I love to dream big and take bold risks. But, if those dreams aren't God's plan for my life, then I don't want those dreams. If we aren't walking in the Lord's purpose for our life, then we are guaranteed to end up wanting and feeling unfulfilled. Our desire should always be to pursue Christ. When we are close with him, we will know what paths to take, what words to say, and what prayers to pray.

Life is full of disruption and stumbles, but we can rest knowing that the Lord's purpose prevails. How can we know the Lord's purpose over our own plans for our life? Spend time with Jesus. Worship Jesus. Talk to Jesus. Talk to people about Jesus. Read his Word. Talk to people about his Word. Consume ourselves with the things he is concerned about. Serve. Love.

Reflect

Tell Jesus the plans of your heart.
Listen to what he tells you in return.

*I pray you will continue to reveal your will over my life, Lord.
Direct my path. Amen.*

Blessed Is She

"Blessed is she who has believed that the Lord
would fulfill his promises to her!"

LUKE 1:45 NIV

Jewish thinkers explain that to bless means to increase in joy, in peacefulness. Jesus tells us the way to be blessed is to believe that God will fulfill his promises to those who believe. Belief has got to come before blessing, sweet sister.

God wants to bless us. Blessing is not something we simply receive; it is a state of being. I am blessed because I know in my heart that God will fulfill what he has promised me. Jesus made promises to us through his Word. We know these promises, we claim these promises, and we believe we will see them in our life. That is living with joy and peacefulness. That is living blessed.

Reflect

What promises has God given you? Spend time today telling him that you believe him and the promises in his Word.

Lord, thank you for your promises over me. I know you are working all things for good. I know you have plans for my future of hope. I believe you know me and love me, and I love you, Jesus. Amen.

Everything New

The one sitting on the throne said, "Look, I am making
everything new!" And then he said to me, "Write this down,
for what I tell you is trustworthy and true."

REVELATION 21:5 NLT

The book of Revelation is the last book of the Bible, and
Jesus declares in it that he will make everything new in the
end. Decay, death, destruction, heartache, and evil are all
part of life on earth, but a time is coming when that will not
be the case. Christ will make all things new, not just for us
but for the whole world.

In the meantime, we know that we are created new in
Jesus. The old self has passed away, and Christ sees us pure
as snow. There are always seasons within our life when God
calls us to another level. We are constantly created anew
when we align our identity in Jesus.

Reflect

Think about the season of life you are in right now.
How have you been made new, and how is
God calling you to your next level?

Jesus, thank you for calling me deeper and deeper. Amen.

Shine Your Light

Neither do people light a lamp and put it under a bowl.
Instead they put it on its stand, and it gives light to everyone
in the house. In the same way, let your light shine before
others, that they may see your good deeds and glorify your
Father in heaven.

MATTHEW 5:15–16 NIV

Let. Your. Light. Shine. God loves glory, and he wants your
talents to shine so that people will see Christ shine through
you. God will be glorified by your boldness, obedience,
faith, and consistency. Your faith will inspire others if you let
your light shine. Don't be afraid to reflect his goodness and
faithfulness.

We should talk about God's provision in our life. We
should tell our friends how God touched our heart at church
or through his Word. We must not hide our faith but let it
shine, for our light gives light to everyone in the house.

Reflect

Let your light shine today. Be intentional about pointing
someone to Jesus with your words and deeds today.

*Lord, thank you for speaking to me in my life. I pray for
opportunities to share you and give you glory. Amen.*

Be Agreed

Can two walk together,
except they be agreed?

AMOS 3:3 KJV

We walk with Jesus every day, but sometimes we choose not to walk in agreement with him. We allow gossip, insecurity, bitterness, and other earthly viewpoints to dictate our mind. But no one can force us to have a bad attitude. Misery is always an option and a choice. Our circumstances, unmet desires, or bad days don't make us bitter. We either choose misery, or we choose to walk with Jesus during the storms, bad days, and trials.

When we walk in agreement with Jesus, heaven can be our reality. That's why we must be of the same spirit as Jesus. What an honor and privilege to host heaven in our life. Christ's peace, joy, strength, and power are always available to us.

Reflect

Picture yourself today walking in agreement with Jesus in everything you do. Imagine him at your side and take note of your boldness in words and deeds.

Lord, I agree and surrender to your plan over my life.
My heart's desire is to give you glory in everything I do.
I want to be in agreement with you. Amen.

Be Kind

Be kind to each other, tenderhearted, forgiving one another,
just as God through Christ has forgiven you.

EPHESIANS 4:32 NLT

It has somehow become acceptable to be rude. Take a peek
at the comments section of anyone with a platform on social
media, and you will see that kindness is scarce these days.
Driving around town, it's clear that other drivers are not
super tenderhearted to one another or even to pedestrians.
We seem to have lost accountability for our actions when we
think it's appropriate to be unkind.

I believe that we are better than that. We follow a
different code of ethics in which we treat people with
kindness. We treasure strangers, and we respect one another.
Let's promise to not find offense so easily as we go about our
days. Let's remember who Christ created us to be and act
that way.

Reflect

Be kind today. Go out of your way to be tenderhearted,
forgiving, and full of grace to whomever Jesus places
in your path.

*Lord, you are the shining example of kindness. I want to
glorify your kindness by showing it to others. Amen.*

Walk with Integrity

The LORD God is a sun and shield; the LORD gives grace and glory; He withholds no good thing from those who walk with integrity.

PSALM 84:11 NASB

Christ withholds no good thing. Now, perhaps you read that and question it a little bit on the inside. I have personally prayed many "good" prayers that went unanswered by God. Am I supposed to believe that I wasn't granted my prayers because of my walk? No. That is not what this verse is saying.

God hasn't held out on me, and he hasn't held out on you. God sees us, and this verse gives us a fresh promise in the midst of our unanswered prayers. He protects us and lights up our life. Because we walk with him in integrity, he withholds no good thing from us. Even when we don't understand, we still have faith because he is God, and we are not.

Reflect

Tell God how you have seen him give you grace and glory lately.

Thank you for loving me, Lord. I praise you for the glory and grace you have poured out onto my life. Amen.

His Peace

Peace I leave you, My peace I give you;
not as the world gives, do I give to you.
Do not let your hearts be troubled, nor fearful.

JOHN 14:27 NASB

Jesus offers us peace, and not just any kind of peace but *his* peace. That doesn't mean we'll have carefree or drama-free lives. We are humans living in the world, and hardships will arise. The difference is that we have access to Jesus' peace. We can have certainty that Christ is King, in control, and working all things for his glory and plan. His plan is good, as he is good. That is why we can have peace that surpasses our understanding.

Jesus charges us to "not let [our] hearts be troubled." And I want to land on the idea that we have control of where we let our hearts dwell. He encourages us not to live in fear but to live in peace. His peace.

Reflect

Read this verse out loud. Then imagine Jesus
speaking it to you personally.

*I will not let my heart be troubled because I trust you, Jesus.
My hope and faith are in you. Amen.*

Guaranteed Blessing

"The LORD will guarantee a blessing on everything you do and will fill your storehouses with grain. The LORD your God will bless you in the land he is giving you."

DEUTERONOMY 28:8 NLT

How amazing is it to be assured that God guarantees to bless us! This promise is very black and white. He wants to bless us in the land he gives us. As we read his Word, the Holy Spirit guides us, and we choose to obey and walk faithfully where Christ has called us.

We have free will and can choose to chase the desires of our heart. But when our desires align with God's call on our life, prepare the storehouse, sweet friend! Blessings upon blessing are guaranteed.

Reflect

Think about the "land" that God is giving you in this season of your life. Talk to Jesus about it. Thank him for aligning your dreams with his.

Lord, I praise your name. I see your fingerprints all over my life, and I am so thankful. Thank you for including me in showcasing your glory. You are so good, Jesus. Amen.

His Voice

By the word of the LORD the heavens were made,
and all the host of them by the breath of His mouth.

PSALM 33:6 NKJV

It is important for us to be reminded of who God is. Our God is powerful and mighty. He creates things merely by speaking them into existence. The breath of his mouth hosts the world. It gives us life. What a beautiful image.

We don't know what God looks like, but we know his voice. John 1:1 tells us, "In the beginning was the Word, and the Word was with God, and the Word was God" (NIV). God is his Word, and he uses his words to create. We can create a better world with our words too. We can use them to build up others, create healthy environments, and dream.

Reflect

Be mindful today of how you use your voice. Notice what you create with the words you choose to use.

Thank you for creating this beautiful world, God. I see your power all around me. You are powerful and amazing, and I bow down before you. Amen.

Live in Freedom

Let's just go ahead and be what we were made to be, without enviously or pridefully comparing ourselves with each other, or trying to be something we aren't.

ROMANS 12:4–6 MSG

Comparison is the thief of joy. That's why we are called to stay in our own lanes and not compare ourselves to others. When we pursue the doors that we know God is opening for us, his blessings follow. As we take bold steps in faith for Jesus, his glory and favor fall upon us.

God wants to use you for his kingdom gain. He uniquely designed you to accomplish things he means specially for you. Step into who he created you to be. Be who you were meant to be. Live in the freedom of who you are, friend.

Reflect

Shine your light today. Don't dim the passions you carry inside of you. They are gifts from God himself!

Jesus, thank you for creating me just the way I am. You have wonderfully made me, and I want to live in the freedom of who I am in you. I praise you for your faithfulness and goodness. Amen.

Thirsty

They did not thirst when he led them through the deserts;
he made water flow for them from the rock;
he split the rock and water gushed out.

ISAIAH 48:21 NIV

In the Bible, the desert is often a metaphor for hardship. We all experience seasons of hardships. Life can be brutal, and some days just seem downright unfair. However, this promise today is gold. God will make water flow for us even if he has to use a rock.

Nowadays, the word *thirsty* is slang for wanting attention. This certainly wasn't what the author intended when he wrote this verse. Because God is our portion, our prize, we aren't called to be thirsty. He is always the source of our fullness and freedom. I pray this image of water gushing in a desert ignites your faith and comforts you today, sweet sister.

Reflect

How are you thirsty in your life right now,
using either definition. Talk to God about that.

*Lord, you provide everything I could ever need.
I worship you. Amen.*

Escape Worry

Set your minds on things that are above,
not on things that are on earth.
COLOSSIANS 3:2 ESV

We read Colossians 3:2 in February, but this time I want to apply it within the context of worry. Worry is circular. It goes around and around in our heads but never leads us anywhere. The Bible reminds us to set our thoughts on things above and to take them captive wherever our minds wander. That means we need to work, ladies! We need to put on our armor every day and open our eyes to the battle around us. We must tackle worry head-on so that we can live in freedom. We mustn't be complacent. We must look up.

Stop letting the cycle of worry blur your vision. God, the Creator of the universe, is all around you. He goes before you, behind you, beside you, and above you. We must train our minds to escape the cycle of worry and focus on things above—the things of eternity, the business of our Father.

Reflect

Set your mind right today.

Thank you for an eternal perspective, Lord.
I want to be what you are about. I set my mind, my sight,
and my focus on you today, Father. Amen.

A Sword

> "Do not suppose that I have come to bring peace to the earth. I did not come to bring peace, but a sword."
>
> MATTHEW 10:34 NIV

At first glance, our verse today may appear to be a contradiction. Jesus is known as the Prince of Peace, yet here he is saying he doesn't come to bring peace but a sword. How do we reconcile the two?

The word *sword* that Jesus used here is the same word used to describe the Word of God: "The word of God is… sharper than any double-edged sword" (Hebrews 4:12 NIV). What Jesus is saying is that the Word of God will divide people, and we see that all around us today. But his Word gives us internal and eternal peace even if it makes people uncomfortable. This is what I love about God's Word. It encourages us to dig deep, and in the pursuit, we see God's glory even more.

Reflect

Have you watered down your convictions
to make others feel comfortable? Why?

*Lord, you are the Prince of Peace. Your Word is powerful,
and I trust you. Amen.*

God Declares

I declare from the beginning how it will end and foretell from the start what has not yet happened. I decree that my purpose will stand, and I will fulfill my every plan.

ISAIAH 46:10 TPT

"My purpose will stand," declares the Lord. God doesn't just speak, he declares. He declared the world into existence. He is full of power, and his plan will stand. It will be fulfilled. Every part of it. How? This is where our faith comes into play. Not every part of this world may be on track, but we can find peace knowing that we have the hope of Jesus.

We tend to change our minds and be indecisive, but God is the same yesterday, today, and forever. We know he is working all things for his glory, and he won't miss a single thing or overlook even the smallest of details. He declares that his purpose will stand, and we can stand on that truth with absolute certainty.

Reflect

Praise God today for his purpose and plan over your life.

I praise you for your plan, Lord. Your ways are higher than mine. I trust your purpose and submit to your will. Amen.

Words

The tongue has the power of life and death,
and those who love it will eat its fruit.

PROVERBS 18:21 NIV

Women tend to talk more than men. It's a fact that, on average, women use more words in a day. We like to discuss our feelings and sometimes the feelings of everyone else around us. This can be a blessing and a curse. Our words shape our life, and sometimes sharing those words can tear down relationships. Just as God spoke the world into existence, our words speak the world around us into existence.

We can choose to lift people up or tear them down. We can choose to gossip or edify. We can choose to compliment or compare. Our words bring us life and death, and they carry power, so let's use that power for God's purpose, kingdom, and glory.

Reflect

Today, choose to be intentional with your words and use them to further the kingdom of heaven.

Lord, my desire is to further your kingdom and build up those around me. Help me choose edifying, loving words. Amen.

Facts

"Here is a boy with five small barley loaves and two small
fish, but how far will they go among so many?"

JOHN 6:9 NIV

The facts of this verse tell us that there is no humanly
possible way for five loaves and two fish to feed five
thousand people. But God is not bound by our limitations.
He is our Creator who is capable of anything, and this verse
is a shining example of how God is beyond our numbers,
facts, and minds. God operates in the domain of the unseen.
Miracles are his specialty.

Do you live your life based on earthly facts and the
seen, or do you take risks when God tells you to step out in
faith? God cannot show us how big his plans are if we try to
confine him to our limited human expectations.

Reflect

Leave room today for God to move. Keep your eyes open to
see him show up for you in ways both big and small.

*I stand in awe of the miracles you perform, Lord. I trust your
will and your power. Thank you for your Word. Amen.*

Pray

Is anyone among you in trouble?
Let them pray.

JAMES 5:13 NIV

If I'm being totally honest, when I am in trouble, my go-to is not to pray. I call. I call my husband, my mom, or my best friend. Prayer is maybe number four on my list. I try to solve the problem, talk about the problem, and then talk about my plan for solving the problem. Then I'll pray. Prayer is not my first response, but this verse inspires me to reorganize my go-to list.

I used to tell people who were in trouble, "I'll pray for you." It's sweet, and I always meant it sincerely, but now I understand that it's a cop-out. Instead, I have started asking, "Can I pray for you?" And if they say yes, then I pray for them with them right then and there. If it's on the phone or even in passing, I stop and pray for them. If we believe in the power of prayer, we should make that our first stop when trouble comes.

Reflect

Get in the habit of prayer. Pray today with someone you know is in need of some prayer.

Thank you, Lord, for your Holy Spirit.
I want to spend time with you. Amen.

Allied with Jesus

You adulterers! Don't you realize that friendship with the
world makes you an enemy of God? I say it again:
If you want to be a friend of the world,
you make yourself an enemy of God.

JAMES 4:4 NLT

Do we live our lives trusting the world? I would argue yes,
we do, most of the time. That would make the world our
friend and, therefore, make us an enemy to God.

God's kingdom and the world's kingdom are opposites
and in constant conflict with one another. We must be on
guard and constantly aware of what we are letting into our
minds, eyes, ears, and souls. We want to be allied with Jesus,
not this world, so we must make a mindful decision not to
befriend it.

Reflect

Make yourself a friend of God today
in all that you say, do, and think.

Jesus, I choose you. Amen.

Heavenly Counselor

I will instruct you and teach you in the way you should go;
I will counsel you with my loving eye on you.

PSALM 32:8 NIV

Life and its uncertainties are out of our control, which can leave many of us feeling a little confused or stressed. But today's promise offers so much comfort. Knowing that the Lord will instruct us in the way we should go gives us peace. Being confident that Jesus is watching over us gives us comfort. The idea that his loving eye is on us makes us feel safe.

The Lord teaches us through life's stressful moments. Our circumstances may not change, but the shift of our focus does. Instead of frustration and fear, we can choose faith and peace.

Reflect

Ask God to teach and counsel you today in the choices you make. Open your eyes to see the Lord moving.

Lord, thank you for your counsel. I know you are bigger than the obstacles I am facing. I trust you. Amen.

Ransomed

O Jacob, listen to the LORD who created you. O Israel, the
one who formed you says, "Do not be afraid, for I have
ransomed you. I have called you by name; you are mine."

ISAIAH 43:1 NLT

The definition of *ransom* is "to free from captivity or
punishment by paying a price." Jesus has released us not
only from death but also from the chains and captivity of
this world. He desires us to live a life full of freedom, for we
belong to God. We don't belong to this world.

The Lord calls you by your name. He knows you and
loves you. He has plans for you, for he created you. If we
remind ourselves of the truth of God's grace and love instead
of the constant stream of fear and discontentment, we can
lead that life of freedom. Our verse today is full of hope and
power if we boldly proclaim it with our mouths and believe
it in our souls.

Reflect

Say this verse out loud, changing the names of Jacob and
Israel to your name.

*Lord, I am not afraid. Thank you for creating me and
calling me by name. Amen.*

God Will Provide

Isaac spoke up and said to his father Abraham, "Father?"
"Yes, my son?" Abraham replied.
"The fire and wood are here," Isaac said, "but where is the lamb for the burnt offering?"
Abraham answered, "God himself will provide the lamb for the burnt offering, my son."
And the two of them went on together.

GENESIS 22:7–8 NIV

This is from the famous story of Abraham when God was testing his faith. Abraham trusted that God would provide, even if it meant he had to choose God over his own son, Isaac. Later, we learn through Scripture that Abraham believed God would raise Isaac from the dead if Abraham had to sacrifice him (see Hebrews 11:19).

Abraham's trust in God is inspiring. His relationship with the Lord was more important to him than anything on the earth. Abraham knew God was good, faithful, and trustworthy. He was convinced that God was capable of anything, even raising someone from the dead.

Reflect

Use Abraham as a role model of faith and trusting God.

You are a God of provision, Lord.
I have faith and hope in you. Amen.

Choose Jesus

"The one who sent me is with me; he has not left me alone,
for I always do what pleases him."

JOHN 8:29 NIV

We always want to please the Lord, not because we want or expect anything from him but because we love him. We don't have to look far in Scripture to read about how precious to God and loved by God we are.

We know he is always with us and doesn't leave us alone. He is a jealous God, and he will not compete for our attention. He is the only one who is worthy of the throne of our praise. He chooses us, but we must also constantly choose him.

Reflect

Choose Jesus today. Be aware of his constant presence.
Out of your love for him, do what pleases him.

Lord, thank you for your presence.
I choose you today and every day. Amen.

Be Still

"Be still, and know that I am God; I will be exalted among
the nations, I will be exalted in the earth."

PSALM 46:10 NIV

"Be still, and know that I am God." Not think or see or hear
but *know*. The way we can enjoy that certainty is by being
still. Stillness is difficult, especially today, when our culture
celebrates busyness. We're constantly on our phones or
distracted by everything happening around us. But it's in our
stillness and surrender that God shows up. That's how we
draw close to him.

God deserves our praise and our attention. When we
focus on him, we see his power and praise it. God is never
pushy; he waits patiently for us to see his glory. We only have
to be still.

Reflect

Spend time in stillness today, allowing your mind to go to
a place where you know with certainty that God is God.

*You are glorious, God. My soul yearns for you,
and I exalt you. Amen.*

No Excuses

The LORD replied, "Don't say, 'I'm too young,' for you must go wherever I send you and say whatever I tell you. And don't be afraid of the people, for I will be with you and will protect you. I, the LORD, have spoken!"

JEREMIAH 1:7–8 NLT

Jeremiah was called by the Lord to deliver a message. He immediately listed all the reasons why he wasn't up to the task, including that he was "just a child." God shut down his excuses, just as he does to ours today.

When we feel called by God to do something, our minds quickly compile a list of excuses to not answer the call. Reasons why we're not good enough. Don't tell God what you aren't capable of. Instead, declare how capable God is. With God, all things are possible. God resides in us.

Reflect

Identify what God is calling you to do in this season of your life. Declare his capabilities.

Lord, I know you are with me wherever I go. I know you are capable of fulfilling the calling deep in my soul. Amen.

Potter and Clay

You, LORD, are our Father. We are the clay, you are the
potter; we are all the work of your hand.

ISAIAH 64:8 NIV

When we are called to participate in God's plan and purpose,
it is a sign of God's favor. He doesn't put passions, desires,
dreams, and hopes inside of us to make us feel dissatisfied.
Those desires are to fuel us on our path for Christ's plan for us.

God has awesome plans for us, and he wants to do
big things through us, but we have to trust him. It is this
beautiful balancing act of boldness and pursuit with
surrender and trust. We are to remind ourselves that we are
the work of God's hands, not our own. We are not in charge;
we are merely the clay. Let's make ourselves available to be
molded by the potter.

Reflect

Tell God today how you are allowing him to mold you.

*Lord, I am the work of your hands. I submit to your plan for
my life. I trust you. Amen.*

You Will Not Stumble

When you walk, your steps will not be hampered;
when you run, you will not stumble.

PROVERBS 4:12 NIV

The word *hamper* means "to restrict the movement of by
bonds or obstacle." Our path in life is not meant to feel
restricted or restrained. God tells us we can live a life where
we run in freedom.

I have found that God tends to use the seemingly
powerless spaces to display his power. It is when we are
weak that he shows his strength. If we could rely on our
own talents, connections, and work ethics, we would, but
God reigns over all. Do you trust what you know, or do you
trust whom you know? He will not let us stumble.

Reflect

Identify any areas in your life in which your steps feel
hampered or restrained. Take that up with God.

*I give you my life, Lord. I want to glorify you
and walk in freedom with you. Direct my steps,
and I know I will not stumble. Amen.*

August

Chosen People

You are a chosen people, a royal priesthood, a holy nation,
God's special possession, that you may declare the praises of
him who called you out of darkness into his wonderful light.

1 PETER 2:9 NIV

I don't know what type of relationships you have had in your
past or if you have ever felt chosen and special by your loved
ones, but you are. When we feel chosen, we are confident.
We know our value and don't allow people to treat us poorly.
And we treat others with a sense of respect and dignity, for
that is all that is appropriate.

God declares that we are his special, chosen possession.
Our response to that is praise for his holy name. It is time to
interrupt our inner narrative that says anything but the truth
that God speaks over us: we are chosen. We are called out
of the darkness. Let's not allow ourselves to live anywhere
outside of his wonderful light. God chooses you!

Reflect

Spend time today praising God for the wonderful light
he has brought into your life.

*Lord, I am so blessed to be your special possession.
You are my hope and the King of kings. Amen.*

On the Throne

He who was seated on the throne said, "I am making everything new!" Then he said, "Write this down, for these words are trustworthy and true."

REVELATION 21:5 NIV

First of all, let's take a moment today to remind ourselves that God sits on the throne. Not you, not me, not the government, not politicians, not movie stars. God. He is seated on the throne. We must remind ourselves of this simple fact when we start to listen to the world around us and feel tempted by the lies that everything is out of control and fear is the only answer. That is a lie. The Lord is in control.

Let us lean into what God declares on his throne: he is making everything new! Everything. You and me. What a beautiful promise of comfort and hope.

Reflect

What would you like to see made new in your life?
Talk to God about that today.

Lord, I am yours. You sit on the throne of the universe, and I thank you for your trustworthiness and goodness. Amen.

But God

My flesh and my heart may fail, but God is the strength of
my heart and my portion forever.

PSALM 73:26 NIV

Several powerful verses in the Bible contain the phrase "but
God," and they all carry the same amount of glory. I may
fail…but God. You intend for harm…but God. He died…
but God.

God is just and powerful. He is good and personal. He
sees you, knows you, and provides for you. We may feel
hopeless, insecure, anxious, or even downcast, but God. God
is our focus, and even though our situation may warrant
stress, we serve a joyful God, and we can't help but be full of
peace. He is the holy of holies who reigns on high, and even
if our flesh fails us, our God never will.

Reflect

What is your "but God" story? I challenge you
to share it with someone today.

Lord, you are my strength. You are all I need.
Thank you for interrupting my selfish focus and shifting my
view onto things that are eternal. Amen.

Nothing Too Hard

"I am the LORD, the God of all mankind.
Is anything too hard for me?"

JEREMIAH 32:27 NIV

God looks for surrender and faith, not perfection. We can ask God to help with our unbelief, and he will pour faith down on our hearts. Nothing is too hard for him. And the more time we spend with God, the more we are united with his heart and Spirit.

When we focus on God, we can walk on water. We can experience miracles if we only believe. We want to live a life of adventure with Jesus, and I can think of no greater adventure than the one God has in store for us.

Reflect

Spend time in prayer today, confessing to the Lord what you have been trying to control out of your lack of faith in him.

You are in control, Lord. Nothing is too hard for you or outside your domain. I trust you with all the struggles on my heart and stressors on my mind. I worship you. Amen.

Prayer Warriors

"All those the Father gives me will come to me,
and whoever comes to me I will never drive away."

JOHN 6:37 NIV

I used to feel insecure about my prayer time. I admired
other believers in the church and figured their prayers
were somehow holier or better than mine. I knew I loved
studying God's Word, and I felt connected to Jesus that way,
so I assumed prayer just wasn't my strong suit. What a lie
that was! Thankfully, I have been set free from that way of
thinking, and I've experienced such freedom in my prayer
life by realizing the words Jesus tells us here.

God loves our prayers whenever we come to him and
in whatever way we do that. He isn't judging us and will
never condemn us as a way of drawing us closer to him. He
will never be dissatisfied by the way we pray. We are prayer
warriors, sister!

Reflect

Pray with the confidence of a prayer warrior today.

*Lord, I love you. I draw near to you, and I thank you
for drawing near to me. Amen.*

Wisdom

Wisdom is sweet to your soul. If you find it, you will have a bright future, and your hopes will not be cut short.

PROVERBS 24:14 NLT

How do we gain wisdom? Reading, researching, and listening, but I would argue that a primary way to gain wisdom is through relationships. Jesus was all about relationships. God is all about relationships. And we get to choose the people we surround ourselves with. We get to choose the podcasts we listen to and the church we attend. The people around us can pour wisdom into us and give us a bright future of joy and hope.

We, too, can be sources of wisdom to other people. We can use the things that God is doing in our life to encourage, inspire, and elevate those around us.

Reflect

Pour into a relationship with someone you admire. Send her a text, asking her to get coffee or to go on a walk. Be wise and intentional about the relationships you are pouring into.

Lord, thank you for putting people in my life whom I look up to. I pray they will pour wisdom into me and that it will be sweet to my soul. Amen.

Justified and Glorified

Those he predestined, he also called;
those he called, he also justified;
those he justified, he also glorified.

ROMANS 8:30 NIV

We are not meant to feel aimless or without direction. God means for our circumstances, talents, passions, and gifts all to work together for his greater purpose. He calls each of us, knows each of us, and has a purpose for each of us. He always wants us to be growing and yet resting in his presence.

I love how our verse today ends with, "Those he justified, he also glorified." When we are justified, it means we are righteous in the eyes of God. To be glorified means God makes us "glorious by bestowing honor, praise, or admiration." God sees you and me as righteous and special. Let's start living in that reality.

Reflect

Do you feel like God is justifying you and thereby glorifying you? Talk to and praise God for that concept.

Lord, thank you for having a special plan and purpose for my life. I trust your ways and submit all my hopes and dreams to you. Amen.

Judge Correctly

> "Stop judging by mere appearances,
> but instead judge correctly."
>
> JOHN 7:24 NIV

Everything isn't what it seems. Instagram lives and perfectly curated grids bombard us, but behind the squares is messy. Just because something looks beautiful doesn't mean that it is. This is counterculture, where everything is accepted and "you do you" is encouraged.

Jesus ends his thought with "judge correctly." That means we must know how to separate good from evil so that we can, in fact, judge correctly. Thankfully, God looks at people's hearts, and we are called to look at the things of eternity and to cling to those things. We want strong spiritual lives, and we want our words to be a blessing. Let's invest more in our quiet time and less on appearances.

Reflect

Judge correctly today.

Thank you for giving me a sound mind, Lord.
I pray my focus will be on things eternal. Amen.

Clutter

A time to search and a time to give up,
a time to keep and a time to throw away.
ECCLESIASTES 3:6 NIV

What do you have in your life that you need to throw away? Emotional baggage? Harmful relationships? Physical stuff that you need to just purge? Hoarding is a way we hold on to the past. We rely on our "stuff" to feel important, comforted, or even in control.

To enter a new season of life, we have to throw away some of the clutter to make space for what God has in store for us. When we hold on to less than God's plan for us, we lower our lives. Let's choose what God has planned for us, not what we think is best. God's plan is always better than our own.

Reflect

What are you holding on to in your life right now that you need to let go? If that means cleaning out your closet, forgiving yourself, or purging old routines, do that today.

*Lord, I want what you have planned for my life,
and I have open arms. Amen.*

Peace and Prayer

Do not be anxious about anything, but in every situation,
by prayer and petition, with thanksgiving, present your
requests to God. And the peace of God, which transcends all
understanding, will guard your hearts and your minds
in Christ Jesus.

PHILIPPIANS 4:6–7 NIV

We live in a time when anxiety is all around us. How can
we step into a life of freedom and peace in all situations? By
prayer. By spending time with our Creator. If we shift our
focus away from all our stress and angst and meditate on
God, peace comes over us in the midst of anxiety.

As we remind ourselves that God sees, knows, and loves
us, our minds become guarded from the dramas of this
world. As we ponder how big and vast and powerful God is,
our problems seem less out of control. The presence of God
diffuses all darkness inside us.

Reflect

Find peace in prayer today.

*I trust you even when my life doesn't make sense, Lord.
I know you are good and mighty. Amen.*

Kingdom of God

Seek ye first the kingdom of God, and his righteousness;
and all these things shall be added unto you.

MATTHEW 6:33 KJV

We can't give what we don't have. If you are trying to pour love and encouragement over others, then that has to come from an overflow of what you possess in your heart. For example, if you are trying to teach kids about forgiveness but you are modeling bitterness, then they won't understand what true forgiveness looks like.

As we seek God and the things of God's hearts, we will be filled with the Lord's presence, and the fruit of that relationship will flow out from us. Out of our relationship with him will flow the light of God. If we seek God first, then the rest of our life will fall into place.

Reflect

Be mindful of God's presence in every situation today.

*Lord, I want my focus to always be on you and your kingdom.
Create in me a pure heart after yours. Amen.*

By Faith

It was by faith that Noah built a large boat to save his family from the flood. He obeyed God, who warned him about things that had never happened before. By his faith Noah condemned the rest of the world, and he received the righteousness that comes by faith.

HEBREWS 11:7 NLT

Noah was obedient, and he was patient. He was building a boat in a drought, and I'm sure there were days when the whole town laughed at him. He was called to condemn the world, but it's safe to assume that the world gladly condemned him in return.

Nevertheless, Noah was faithful. He knew God had called him to build a boat, and that's exactly what he did. Noah had big faith, and it led him to big things.

Reflect

Spend time in prayer today asking God for big faith. Talk to him about how you trust him and how you have seen him come through for you in the past.

I desire the righteousness that comes by faith.
I will go where you lead me, Lord. Help my unbelief
and increase my faith. Amen.

Yesterday, Today, and Forever

*Jesus Christ is the same yesterday
and today and forever.*

Hebrews 13:8 esv

When you read the Word of God, the same Spirit that was present when the words were written is present today. Despite culture shifting, customs changing, and ways of thinking evolving, God and his Word remain the same. The truth is the truth is the truth. It doesn't change.

Like his Word, God is consistent, and as we study his character through his Word, we find that he never contradicts himself. We must be careful not to mistake God's mystery as inconsistency. He offers to us the same promises that God proclaimed to the people in the Bible. Our job is to take hold of those promises and walk in a life of freedom. Sometimes God doesn't do things the way we think he should, but we trust our everlasting Father, for he reigns yesterday, today, and forever.

Reflect

Take time to reflect on your faith walk so far. Tell God how he has consistently demonstrated his character and love for you.

*Lord, you are the same yesterday, today, and forever.
I find comfort in who you are. Continue to reveal
yourself to me. Amen.*

He Will Do It

The one who calls you is faithful,
and he will do it.

1 Thessalonians 5:24 NIV

I am a doer. I don't like meetings where people sit around and talk about what they are going to do. I like to do it and then figure out how I might have messed up along the way. My husband is the opposite. He likes to plan, plan, plan. Naturally, to keep things interesting, we are not only life partners but also business partners. After more than fifteen years of happy marriage, we have come to learn that, despite our differences, we balance each other out.

We need a similar kind of balance with God. We can't just sit on our couch and expect God to make all our dreams come true. We have to take bold steps of faith and then watch God move mountains. He is faithful, and he won't bring you to something if he isn't planning to bring you through it.

Reflect

Claim "he will do it" every time worry, doubt,
or anxiety starts to rise up in you today.

*You will do it, Lord. You are faithful,
and I trust you. Amen.*

Mysterious

There is a God in heaven who reveals mysteries.

DANIEL 2:28 NIV

I love the boldness that this verse holds. God will pour down wisdom to us if we are ready to listen to him. Stress, busyness, worry, all these things hinder our souls from hearing from our maker. God wants to reveal the great adventure and promised land that he has planned for us. However, we do not serve a pushy God. He waits patiently, and sometimes we become so distracted that he never has an opportunity to reveal great wisdom to us.

Have you felt like God has revealed secrets to you? Have you ever read a Bible verse and felt confused, but as you took the time to research and understand it, you discovered a life-changing truth? God wants to whisper to us. He wants a great love story with you and me.

Reflect

Say our verse out loud to someone today and make space to allow God to reveal mysteries to you.

Lord, you reveal mysteries. Share your wisdom with me.
As I draw near to you, allow me to feel you
draw near to me, Jesus. Amen.

Dreams

If you wait for perfect conditions,
you will never get anything done.

ECCLESIASTES 11:4 TLB

As our verse today explains, our dreams can never come true if we wait around for the perfect conditions. We are followers of Jesus, so we are called to be easygoing yet determined. Full of love yet living in the light. Expectant, yet full of surrender. We see this balance in Christ, as Jesus is King, yet he came to serve. You were made for this season, this point in time, this location, with your specific talents, influence, and gifts. Everything is God-ordained for his glory.

Let's turn our faces to heaven and focus our eyes on Jesus. He guides us in the way we should go. We walk in boldness, with our hands open but our vision laser-focused on he who sent us.

Reflect

What is something that you have been waiting for? Perhaps now is the time to take a step of boldness and faith.

Lord, thank you for giving me hopes and dreams.
Thank you for transforming my heart. Amen.

Fix Your Gaze

Let your eyes look straight ahead;
fix your gaze directly before you.

PROVERBS 4:25 NIV

Do you ever feel like everything is a mess? Like you're striving for organization and perfection or a consistent routine for your family, but you just feel out of sorts and less than? When these feelings come, that's when we need to shift our perspective. We need to see our situation and the world around us through the lens of Jesus.

Sometimes a higher point of view is all we need to see our calling clearly. A different outlook allows us to see the distractions in our life for what they are and remove anything that takes us away from our purpose. As Jesus put it in Matthew 6:34, "Do not worry about tomorrow, for tomorrow will worry about itself" (NIV). Let's focus on what lies directly ahead of us, friend.

Reflect

Fix your gaze today on what is directly before you.

You are my focus, Lord. I love you. Amen.

Such a Time as This

"If you remain silent at this time, relief and deliverance for the Jews will arise from another place, but you and your father's family will perish. And who knows but that you have come to your royal position for such a time as this?"

ESTHER 4:14 NIV

The story of Esther is worth studying. She was an orphan and a foreigner, but she was able to rise in rank and gain a royal position in the palace of her day. God called Esther to step up and speak out on behalf of the Jews, but to enter the king's court without permission was an offense punishable by death. But Esther used her voice, saved her people, and became queen.

Esther's story is a perfect example of how God is in control. He invites us to join in on his plan, and many times, that requires boldness. We will feel fear, but we claim our faith and rest on the knowledge that God has made us "for such a time as this."

Reflect

What do you feel God is calling you to do in your life right now? Name it and claim it!

Thank you, Lord, for inviting me into your plan.
I pray that I will act boldly like Esther and use my voice
according to your will. Amen.

Higher Calling

From the ends of the earth I call to you, I call as my heart
grows faint; lead me to the rock that is higher than I.

PSALM 61:2 NIV

God is always calling us higher and deeper. Sometimes we
can feel his presence strongly and hear his voice clearly. It
seems wherever we go, we can't escape the message that he is
trying to teach us. Other times, we feel isolated and far from
the Lord, and his presence seems hard to find.

No matter the season we find ourselves in, we call to
Jesus. He is always with us and always has a plan for us. He
never leaves us or forsakes us. He uses different methods
to encourage our faith and grow our trust in him, but he is
never finished working on us and calling us to new levels in
every aspect of our life.

Reflect

Think about how God is guiding you toward him.
Are you following his lead?

*Lord, you are the Rock in my life that is higher than anything
else. Thank you for pursuing me. I call to you. Amen.*

Spiritual Maturity

"The Lord disciplines the one he loves,
and chastises every son whom he receives."

HEBREWS 12:6 ESV

God instructs those he loves. He corrects us when we make mistakes and uses those opportunities to develop spiritual growth in our faith journey. Our spiritual maturity can come from beautiful experiences, but many times it will come from painful times. He disciplines us to grow.

As believers, we shouldn't respond to hardships with bitterness or despair. We aren't in heaven yet, so we will experience hurt and pain. Remember that God has a plan, and he is engaged in our life. It is never fun to be in the fire, but what comes out is always precious and full of beauty. That's the stuff God is after.

Reflect

Reflect on how you respond to hardship. Do you blame God and grow doubtful and bitter, or do you cling to God and trust him in the storm?

*Thank you for taking an active role in my life, Lord.
I know you use everything to mold me
into who you created me to be. Amen.*

Crossroads

This is what the LORD says: "Stand at the crossroads and look; ask for the ancient paths, ask where the good way is, and walk in it, and you will find rest for your souls."

JEREMIAH 6:16 NIV

Resting is holy. We need to have rest in our life. Rest in our bodies, rest in our minds, and rest in our souls. How miraculous does that sound? It is attainable, even when we are at a crossroads. Usually, when I have to make a decision and I'm feeling confused, that is the prime time that I feel anxious. Rest seems so far out of my reach. But our verse today tells us to ask which path to take and then to find rest in our souls.

I find that prayer is intertwined with rest. The more I pray about something, even if it doesn't go the way I prayed, I have a sense of peace and rest. I feel confident that I have handed that thing over to the Lord, and therefore I trust that God has it. I have rest in my soul.

Reflect

Allow yourself to rest today.

Guide me, Lord, and lead me to rest in my soul. Amen.

Tempted in Every Way

We do not have a high priest who cannot sympathize with our weaknesses, but One who has been tempted in all things just as we are, yet without sin.

HEBREWS 4:15 NASB

The author of Hebrews is not suggesting that Jesus was tested in every way that we are. He was alive at a different time, so his life looked different from someone living in our modern society. However, the author is offering encouragement, noting that Jesus, who was fully God yet fully man, understands our temptations. Jesus himself was tempted, yet he withheld and stood strong against the temptation.

Jesus understands our struggle. He can empathize with our weakness because he was a human who lived in the world. Yes, he was blameless, but he, too, was tempted.

Reflect

Do you think of Jesus as a God who understands your struggles? Allow him to empathize with you today.

Lord, you know my struggles, my doubts, and my fears. You have a plan for me and my life. I cling to you, Lord. Amen.

Joy of His Presence

You will show me the way of life, granting me the joy of your presence and the pleasures of living with you forever.

PSALM 16:11 NLT

Meeting with God is joyful. We bring our requests, prayers, and burdens to the throne of our God, but he also offers us the sheer joy of his presence. Worshiping God makes our souls shine. Our faces feel radiant, and appreciating his creation and beauty all around us gives us a sense of hope and rest.

We must create space for our souls to find joy by focusing on his presence. Yes, his Spirit is always with us, but we can distract ourselves and busy our days so much that we end up missing him. Jesus was always on a mission but never too busy to stop and take time for whomever or whatever crossed his path. Let's follow our Savior's example.

Reflect

Set aside time today to find joy in God's presence.

Lord, thank you for everlasting life and the joy of your presence. Amen.

Arise and Shine

Arise, shine, for your light has come,
and the glory of the Lord has risen upon you.
ISAIAH 60:1 ESV

What a powerful verse we read today. We shine, for the glory of the Lord has risen on us. Have you ever wondered what the "glory of the Lord" means? Glory is the manifestation of God's beauty.

God bestows on us all things because of his goodness. He is a generous God who even shares his glory with us so that we can shine it upon others. I love to take his Word and dissect the message that the writer is communicating. God's Word is full of tender love and goodness. We serve a good, good Father. What a gift!

Reflect

Turn your focus to God and his glory shining through you today. Let the Lord reveal to you what that means, perhaps through his Word or his presence.

Lord, I praise you for your glory. You are beautiful, and you shine so brightly in my life. I see you moving through me and all around me. I invite you into this place.
Come, Lord Jesus, come! Amen.

Worth

Each person is given something to do that shows who God is: Everyone gets in on it, everyone benefits. All kinds of things are handed out by the Spirit, and to all kinds of people!

1 Corinthians 12:4–11 MSG

You are gifted. You are talented. Your identity is rooted in Jesus, and no mean comments on Instagram, no gossip about you, no number on the scale, and no brand of clothes determines your worth or identity.

We are set free from striving when we find our identity in Jesus. Once we know our worth, our gifts begin to blossom, and we reflect God's qualities through those gifts that he has given us. God doesn't set us free and give us talents for ourselves. We are made to share them with the world.

Reflect

Write down four of your gifts. How are you using them to help others and glorify God? If you aren't, think of how you can start using them today.

Lord, thank you for blessing me. I want to glorify you with my gifts and talents. Open the doors you want me to walk through. I pray for your favor over my life. Amen.

Walk in Truth

I have no greater joy than to hear that
my children are walking in the truth.

3 John 1:4 NIV

God's truth has more power to set you free than your truth, which leaves you in bondage. Read that again because those are not my words; those are from the Holy Spirit. God knows and sees our true selves. He sent his Son to set us free, not just from the chains of death but also from the bondages of this life.

Perhaps your past decisions have given you a false sense of self. Perhaps your "truth" believes you aren't good enough, smart enough, beautiful enough, or whatever enough. That is simply a lie. God's truth is more powerful and real, and it breaks the chain of lies that we get trapped in. And you know what? Nothing delights our Lord more than when we walk and live in his truth.

Reflect

What lies do you believe to be true in your life?
Ask God to reveal one to you today.

I want to walk in your truth, Lord. Set me free, Jesus! Amen.

Talents versus Gifts

Every good and perfect gift is from above,
coming down from the Father of the heavenly lights,
who does not change like shifting shadows.

JAMES 1:17 NIV

I have been studying the difference between gifts and talents. Our talents are things that we are naturally good at, and we can probably hide them if we choose to. We can form our identity around our talents or even make them our idols.

Gifts, on the other hand, are the things God has created us to do. He gives us spiritual gifts. For example, you can tell if it's someone's gift to lead worship or preach or teach Sunday school. Yes, we can practice and become better at anything we put our mind to, but our gifting is where the power of the Holy Spirit comes into play. We can sense God's favor and presence when we are living out what he created us to do.

Reflect

What are your gifts, and what are your talents?

Lord, thank you for blessing me with so much. I want to step into my gifts and use them to bring you glory. Amen.

Perfume

Mary took about a pint of pure nard, an expensive perfume;
she poured it on Jesus' feet and wiped his feet with her hair.
And the house was filled with the fragrance of the perfume.

John 12:3 niv

Mary poured perfume over Jesus during the week that he
would die. This act was far more than a gesture of respect.
In the culture of their day, a woman often saved perfume for
her wedding day, when she would pour it over her husband
as an act of devotion. Mary gave Jesus all that she had. Some
of the disciples in the room considered her a fool, but Jesus
understood her. He saw a devoted woman with a sincere
heart who wanted to offer her devotion to her Savior.

Days later, Jesus knew the cross lay ahead of him, and
he prayed. The Bible records Jesus sweating blood and crying
in the garden. I can't help but wonder if he could still smell
Mary's perfume. Perhaps he was reminded of her love.
Perhaps that gave him comfort or reminded him of why he
had to endure the cross.

Reflect

**What "perfume" can you pour out today
as an act of worship?**

I love you, Lord. Amen.

Dark Times

You have taken from me friend and neighbor—
darkness is my closest friend.

PSALM 88:18 NIV

What do you do in dark times? Do you become angry and run from God? Grow bitter and full of doubt? Do you wrestle with God and bring your hurt and frustrations to his throne? We all feel like life isn't fair sometimes, and we all experience hurt, betrayal, rejection, and disappointment.

I have found that Jesus is always the best example of how to live. What did Jesus do when he felt lost or confused? We read in the gospels that Jesus prayed to God, "May this cup be taken from me" when he was about to endure the cross. He prayed three times for God to change his will, yet he always ended his prayer with "may your will be done" (Matthew 26:39–44 NIV).

Reflect

Be honest with God and tell him what you want.
Then submit to his will.

Jesus, I trust your will over my life and submit to it. Amen.

Light and Joy

The life of the godly is full of light and joy,
but the light of the wicked will be snuffed out.

PROVERBS 13:9 NLT

The Message translates this verse as, "The lives of good people are brightly lit streets." You are a light and a source of joy because of your faith, and you shine for others to see. You stand on holy ground wherever you stand because God has sent you there.

We can snuff out our light if we don't allow God to shine. That's why we must be responsible for our actions and walk in freedom with the truth. Our actions matter. What we do in the quiet, secret places matter, and our consistent acts carry weight. You can play a part in God's story and be a light even in the darkest of places.

Reflect

Be a light today.

*Lord, you are so good. I taste your goodness, and I see.
Thank you for loving me and choosing me.*

Think Strong, Be Strong

Very truly I tell you, it is for your good that I am going away.
Unless I go away, the Advocate will not come to you;
but if I go, I will send him to you.

JOHN 16:7 NIV

So often, we think, *I can't do this*, or *It's too much for me*, but we can do whatever God has called us to do. Jesus gave us his Spirit, and it is always with us. It lives inside us. His Spirit guides us, directs us, and gives us power.

We are heirs to the throne and daughters of the King. If you think you can or think you can't, either way you are going to be right. Think strong and we will be strong. Think weak and we will be weak. We are victorious, so let's think that we can!

Reflect

Think strong today.

I believe I can, Lord! I am ready to do any assignment that you will give me. Amen.

September

One Bold Step

David knew that the LORD had established him as king
over Israel and had exalted his kingdom for the sake
of his people Israel.

2 SAMUEL 5:12 NIV

King David was a shepherd boy who became Israel's third
and arguably most important king. He's the most frequently
mentioned human in the Old Testament and the second-
most mentioned person in the Bible, second to Jesus. David's
calling didn't make sense and was not even feasible by
worldly standards, yet he knew who God called him to be.
He was certain of it.

We all have different seasons. When I had three babies
at home, my calling was very different compared to what I
feel God is guiding me toward now. God never reveals too
much to us, but he always encourages us to take one bold
step in faith at a time. Are you certain where God is calling
you? Have you asked God to reveal his plan for your life?

Reflect

Complete the sentence: I know that
the Lord has called me to…

*Lord, thank you for your plan for my life.
I trust you. Amen.*

Our Shepherd

The LORD is my shepherd; I shall not want. He makes me
to lie down in green pastures; He leads me beside the still
waters. He restores my soul; He leads me in the paths of
righteousness for His name's sake.

PSALM 23:1–3 NKJV

Let's remember that the Lord is our Shepherd. We were lost
but now are found. Addiction, anxiety, loneliness, lack of
self-confidence…none of these chains are meant for you,
sweet sister. God wants to restore our souls and help us live
fulfilled lives.

When we have God, we have it all. Have you fallen in
love with your Creator? The more effort we put into our
relationship with Jesus, the more our life starts to make sense.
God will lead us to green pastures and restore our soul.

Reflect

Read all of Psalm 23 today. Plan to shift your focus from
that of scarcity to that of abundance.

*Lord, you are the Shepherd of my life. I lack nothing when I
have you. Open my eyes to know this truth with all my being.
Amen.*

Obey

Naaman went away angry and said, "I thought that he would surely come out to me and stand and call on the name of the LORD his God, wave his hand over the spot and cure me of my leprosy."

2 KINGS 5:11 NIV

The context behind this story is that Naaman was a commander who had leprosy, and a servant girl who worked in his household believed Elisha the prophet could heal her master. Naaman sought out Elisha to see if he could be healed, and when Naaman arrived at the prophet's door, Elisha sent out a messenger to tell Naaman what he needed to do in order to be healed.

Instead of doing what Elisha instructed, Naaman became angry. He felt that he was stepping out in faith to be healed and expected God to work in a certain way, to simply wave his hand and cure him. We can surely relate to this. Sometimes we take steps of faith for God, and when he doesn't show up the way we want him to, we become angry. What Naaman needed to do was obey. Thankfully, he did as he was told and was indeed cured of his leprosy.

Reflect

Submit to God's will and have faith today.

Lord, you are God, and you have all of my respect.
I strive to obey you today and in the future. Amen.

Storms

The LORD is slow to anger but great in power; the LORD will not leave the guilty unpunished. His way is in the whirlwind and the storm, and clouds are the dust of his feet.

NAHUM 1:3 NIV

I love the middle phrase of this verse: "His way is in the whirlwind and the storm." Sometimes we tend to believe the lie that if we follow God, then our life will be free of storms. Nowhere is that found in the Bible.

What God has promised us is that he will walk through the storms with us. He tells us that he is good, no matter the circumstances. He is trustworthy and reliable. The clouds are like dust to his feet, for he is the mighty Creator of all.

Reflect

How have you seen God's power on display in your life?
Praise God for his power.

You created all that I see, Lord. You are just and mighty, holy and pure. I love you and surrender my storms to you. Amen.

Slow to Anger

My dear brothers and sisters, take note of this: Everyone should be quick to listen, slow to speak and slow to become angry, because human anger does not produce the righteousness that God desires.

JAMES 1:19–20 NIV

I admit that I struggle with anger. I am a hothead and quick to react. I see my sons imitating me and my dysfunctional anger, and I apologize to them. I apologize because I want that bad habit to end with me, not to pass it down to them. It's not how I want to act.

It's easy to justify our shortcomings with excuses like, "I'm Italian…I'm just passionate…It's the way my family acted." But we have to realize that we can't honor God when we are stuck in an emotional state of anger. Not to mention the fact that the stress of carrying anger around takes a toll on our immune system, so we need to let it go for the sake of our own health. Instead, we want to be slow to speak and slow to anger so that we can "produce the righteousness that God desires." Let's be righteous believers.

Reflect

Repeat these phrases to yourself throughout the day as reminders: quick to listen, slow to speak, and slow to anger.

Lord, I want to produce righteousness with my words, deeds, and thoughts. Amen.

Love One Another

"I am giving you a new commandment, that you love one another; just as I have loved you, that you also love one another. By this all people will know that you are My disciples: if you have love for one another."

JOHN 13:34–35 NASB

Our world has so much division today. But when we study God's Word, we see that unity is one of the overarching themes of the New Testament. Perhaps the Bible talks so much about unity because it doesn't come naturally to us. It is a heart issue.

Jesus isn't asking us to show our love by dying for someone like he did for us, but he is asking us to die to ourselves. When we submit to God and dethrone our own sense of pride and entitlement, love shines bright. That is how people will know that we are followers of Christ: by the way we love one another.

Reflect

Let's try not to be easily offended today and to love people, even the ones who don't agree with us.

Lord, I want to be a beacon of light for unity.
I want to focus on the things I have in common with people,
not the things that separate us. Amen.

He Cares

Humble yourselves under the mighty power of God, and at the right time he will lift you up in honor. Give all your worries and cares to God, for he cares about you.

1 Peter 5:6–7 NLT

I like to joke that I'm overconfident because my parents *really* talked me up. They were always impressed by me and cheering me on, so I was convinced I was a rock star at all things. This simply wasn't reality, but it was true for me, and it became my reality. I was bold and fearless. I felt free to be fully me because, in my mind, I believed I was great.

If we live in a state of fear and anxiousness, then our actions will not be bold for Jesus. However, if we know in the deepest part of our soul that God cares for us, then we'll be unstoppable for God's kingdom. Let me tell you today that you are awesome. God has big plans for you in his due time and under his authority. He cares for you. Trust him.

Reflect

Walk today with boldness for Jesus,
knowing God cares for you.

I humble myself before you, God. I know that you care for me, and I give you all my worries and cares. Amen.

Things Above

You have been raised with Christ, set your hearts on things above, where Christ is, seated at the right hand of God. Set your minds on things above, not on earthly things. For you died, and your life is now hidden with Christ in God.

COLOSSIANS 3:1–3 NIV

Some verses are so powerful without even digging, and our passage today is one of those. Without Jesus, our hearts pursue other things, earthly things. Our minds think other things.

This verse is a charge not to live like that. That old self has died, and our new self has been raised with Jesus Christ. We now set our minds on things above, not things of this world. Let the truth of these words fill your Spirit today and encourage your soul.

Reflect

How have your heart and mind changed
since you were raised with Jesus Christ?

*Lord, I set my heart on the things you have a heart for.
I set my mind on things above. Thank you for your Spirit.
Thank you for your love. You are holy. Amen.*

Inner Thoughts

The mob shouted louder and louder, demanding that Jesus be crucified, and their voices prevailed.

LUKE 23:23 NLT

Nails didn't hold Jesus on the cross; his love for us did. As the very people he came to love and save shouted in his face, "Crucify him!" he laid down his life to save their souls for all eternity. He bled and bruised, and bruising is indicative of internal injury. If you recall what we discussed back in February, his external bleeding reflects his forgiveness of our external actions, and his internal bruising reflects his forgiveness of our inner thoughts. He's our external and internal Savior, who took away the sins of the world.

I am not aware of your inner thoughts, but make no mistake, sweet friend, Jesus knows. He knows your hurts, your doubts, and your fears, and I promise you that there is no place you can run that is too dark for Jesus. You are never out of his grasp. He knew our innermost places, and still he lay down his life for us.

Reflect

Spend time thanking God for knowing your innermost thoughts and loving you all the same.

Jesus, I thank you for making the ultimate sacrifice so that I can live forever. Amen.

Die to Ourselves

I am crucified with Christ: nevertheless I live; yet not I, but
Christ liveth in me: and the life which I now live in the flesh
I live by the faith of the Son of God, who loved me,
and gave himself for me.

GALATIANS 2:20 KJV

Our culture has made the self king above all else, pushing
mantras like, "Be true to yourself," "Follow your heart," and
"Embrace your truth." But none of these ideas actually lead
to happiness or fulfillment.

We want to be generous and giving, yet we choose
to buy another sweater we don't really need. We want to
love and support others, but we just can't seem to find the
time. We constantly choose to live in the flesh or to live by
faith. The world tells us to do whatever our heart tells us
to do because the ultimate goal is happiness, but this is the
opposite of the gospel. We are called to die to ourselves and,
instead, to live by the faith of the Son of God.

Reflect

Die to self in three different ways today,
whether that's volunteering your time, resources,
or energy to someone or something else.

I live by faith, Jesus. I choose you.
Increase you and decrease me in my life. Amen.

Exploits

The people that do know their God shall be strong,
and do exploits.

DANIEL 11:32 KJV

This verse in Daniel calls us to know God, be strong, and carry out exploits. An *exploit* is defined as "a notable, memorable, or heroic act." We are created to live like that. Does your life echo boldness? Do you believe the truth about who God created you to be and the things God created you to do, or are you filled with anxiety, fear, and self-doubt?

As we grow closer to Jesus, we become bolder in who we are and what we pursue. Our faith makes us more courageous. It is our choice to rise to the occasion. Let's go!

Reflect

List out all your why-nots. Pray that the Spirit of God will shatter all of your insecurity and self-doubt.

Lord, thank you for planning exploits for my life. I am ready to rise and carry them out for your glory. Amen.

Raised and Seated

Because of his great love for us, God, who is rich in mercy, made us alive with Christ even when we were dead in transgressions—it is by grace you have been saved. And God raised us up with Christ and seated us with him in the heavenly realms in Christ Jesus.

EPHESIANS 2:4–6 NIV

The words used for "raised" and "seated" appear in Greek in the original text of this verse and are presented as a fact. They have already happened. God created time and exists outside of it. It is impossible for us to fully understand, but in God's realm, we are already raised and seated with Jesus in heaven. Our earthly life and eternal destination are rooted in Christ, so we can't earn or lose our seat.

I love that God's grace, mercy, and love are tied into the truths we receive from Jesus. God loves us and has raised us to a new life.

Reflect

From today's Scripture, list every truth that is ours in Jesus.

You are rich in mercy and grace, Lord.
I praise you for your power and love. Amen.

Appearances

Why do you worry about clothes? See how the flowers of the field grow. They do not labor or spin. Yet I tell you that not even Solomon in all his splendor was dressed like one of these. If that is how God clothes the grass of the field, which is here today and tomorrow is thrown into the fire, will he not much more clothe you—you of little faith?

MATTHEW 6:28–30 NIV

I remember being a little girl and reading Jesus' words here and feeling what I now understand as being convicted. I have always loved fashion and expressing my moods through my outfits. I am girlie, and a pretty pair of shoes makes me feel glamorous. Jesus isn't condemning that here, but he is telling us that appearances do not matter.

Like everything, it's a heart issue. Are we putting our identity in our appearance? Are we trusting that God will provide for us? How much more he loves us than the flowers! It will all work out. Let go and let God.

Reflect

Try not to worry today. Exercise trust.

I know that you will provide for me, Jesus, and that I do not need to worry about appearances. I trust you. Amen.

Found

> The angel of the LORD found Hagar near a spring in the desert; it was the spring that is beside the road to Shur.
>
> GENESIS 16:7 NIV

When Hagar found herself in a hard situation and in a hopeless season of her life, she ran away. The verse reads that the Lord "found" her, and in this context, *found* is implying that God specifically sought her out. I love Hagar's story. It's full of God's goodness and provision, and we see his love on display.

I'm sure we can all relate to wanting to run away from life sometimes. But even when we try to run from him, he continually seeks us. He always knows where we are. And even though he may not change our situations or circumstances, he changes our perspective, which gives us the strength to change our situation.

Reflect

Recall a time when you felt God seeking you.
Thank him for that.

Lord, I am found in you, and I am grateful for your love.
Thank you for pursuing me. Amen.

Believe God

Abram believed the LORD,
and he credited it to him as righteousness.

GENESIS 15:6 NIV

To be righteous means to be "morally right or justifiable." Of course, we are not righteous compared to God's perfect nature, but through our belief in Jesus, we are righteous. Belief comes before righteousness, and that belief sets us free. When we believe God, our whole life shifts. Yes, we believe in God, but do we believe God? Do you believe he can do what he has said he can do?

The Bible is full of stories of men and women who take bold steps of faith because they believed God. They may have doubted, attempted to control, or gone astray, yet God continued to pursue them and provide a way back to him. He is good. He sees us, and he speaks to us. We get to choose to believe him or doubt.

Reflect

Choose belief today!

Help me with my unbelief, Lord. I choose you. Help me step out into a bold faith. Transform my heart, my thoughts, and my life, Jesus, for your glory. I am yours. Amen.

Wait upon the Lord

They who wait upon the Lord will get new strength. They will rise up with wings like eagles. They will run and not get tired. They will walk and not become weak.

ISAIAH 40:31 NLV

When we hear the word *wait*, we perhaps picture ourselves just sitting around, doing nothing, and feeling bored. But it can be a misleading word because waiting is actually an action word. We hope, trust, and expectantly watch for God to move.

There is faith in the waiting. And even in the waiting, God is doing big things and taking us to the next level. He gives us strength as we wait, and we rise up. He promises that we will not tire or become weak. Instead, we will run. As we wait, we rise!

Reflect

Meditate on the phrase "Wait in hope on the Lord."
What does that mean to you right now in your life?
Be specific and share your answer with God.

Lord, you are my hope, and I place my trust in you.
Help me rise up with wings like eagles. Amen.

Small Beginnings

"Do not despise these small beginnings,
for the LORD rejoices to see the work begin."
ZECHARIAH 4:10 NLT

There's a lie that many Christians believe to be true: "That's not for me." Or "I could never." The words may vary, but the lie is the same. We can believe that, somehow, we aren't included in God's plan, as if big things aren't meant for us. Sure, small beginnings can feel discouraging to us. We want the success before the work. But the Lord rejoices to see the work begin even in the small things.

Allow me to assure you that God has big plans for us. He wants to use us. We are his arms, hands, voice, and glory on earth today. He chooses everyone, including the misfits and the forgotten, to accomplish the wonderful. Make yourself available to Jesus.

Reflect

What goal or task have you wanted to accomplish but just keep putting off? Take the first step toward accomplishing that today.

*Thank you for using me, Lord. I want to take bold steps,
and I know that you are working behind the scenes.
My call is to be faithful. Your job is to work it all out.
I trust your plans. Amen.*

Safety in the Lord

Fearing people is a dangerous trap,
but trusting the LORD means safety.

PROVERBS 29:25 NLT

Do you care too much about what people think about you?
Women, by nature, tend to be more nurturing and can fall
into the trap of people pleasing. We find ourselves in certain
situations or among certain groups of people that trigger us.
We want them to like us, or we care what they think.

We need to free ourselves from that trap. We must stay
focused on the Lord and what he has called us to do. We are
not man-made; we are God-made. God is responsible for
the way he made us, and we are responsible for what God
has called us to do. Trust God with all of your sensitivities,
dreams, past, passions, insecurities, all of it. In him we are
safe, and he doesn't make mistakes.

Reflect

Thank God for designing you exactly as you are.
Enjoy the safety and security of his presence.

*Lord, thank you for making me perfectly me.
You love me, and I am so grateful. Amen.*

Return with Joy

Those who go out weeping, carrying seed to sow,
will return with songs of joy, carrying sheaves with them.

PSALM 126:6 NIV

When we look through the Bible, we read many stories of God's followers who never received their promised land. Moses never entered the promised land but saw it from afar. Abraham never owned any of his promised land. It's often the path, not the fulfillment of the promise, that brings us the hope and glory of Christ.

Still, the Bible promises that our weeping will be turned into joy. We can hold on to this promise. We can look beyond our struggles and sufferings and know that our tears will produce a harvest of joy. This promise doesn't mean that God will simply make everything okay if we say a prayer and offer our situation to him. However, looking to him to shift our perspective from our problem to our problem solver can bring us joy.

Reflect

Is your hope on the destination or on the journey with Jesus?

You turn my tears to songs of praise with just your presence, Lord. Please move in my life. Amen.

Our Advocate

I will ask the Father, and he will give you another advocate to help you and be with you forever—the Spirit of truth. The world cannot accept him, because it neither sees him nor knows him. But you know him, for he lives with you and will be in you.

JOHN 14:16–17 NIV

Jesus asked God to send his Holy Spirit of truth to live and be in us. We know him. He is truth, and he is for us. He comes alongside us in every difficult situation that we face, empowering and advocating for us. He wants to see us grow and succeed. What a sweet and powerful demonstration of God's power, grace, and love.

Oh, my soul, I could cry just sitting here and thinking of the goodness and faithfulness of God. The Spirit of truth lives in you, sweet sister.

Reflect

Sit in the truth of today's verse.
Thank God for his goodness and love for us.

Jesus, thank you for the Spirit of truth. I know him, and he lives in me. Yes, Lord! Amen.

Marked with a Seal

You also were included in Christ when you heard the message of truth, the gospel of your salvation. When you believed, you were marked in him with a seal, the promised Holy Spirit, who is a deposit guaranteeing our inheritance until the redemption of those who are God's possession— to the praise of his glory.

EPHESIANS 1:13–14 NIV

The seal that Paul is writing about here refers to an official mark or identification, and the moment we believe, we are marked with that seal. It marks us as Christ's, and it signifies security, authenticity, ownership, and authority.

Like we discussed yesterday, the Holy Spirit takes up residence inside of us. The same Spirit that raised Christ from the dead and created the world we see advocates and helps us every moment of our existence. What a concept! What a beautiful and gracious God we serve.

Reflect

Read these verses a little at a time today because there's so much beauty to unpack. Let the truth of these promises change your soul.

How my soul rejoices over you with thanksgiving, Jesus. Praise to the glory of our Father. Amen.

Heavenly Citizenship

Our citizenship is in heaven. And we eagerly await a Savior from there, the Lord Jesus Christ, who, by the power that enables him to bring everything under his control, will transform our lowly bodies so that they will be like his glorious body.

PHILIPPIANS 3:20–21 NIV

We are citizens of heaven, not of this world. Citizenship is gained by "meeting the legal requirements of a national, state, or local government. A nation grants certain rights and privileges to its citizens."[10] Our requirements for heavenly citizenship were met in Jesus.

We believe in him, and the power that enabled him to conquer death will be the same power to transform our bodies into a heavenly form. That is our right and privilege because of our love of Jesus and our faith in him.

Reflect

Do you live like you belong to heaven or to earth?

Jesus, I belong to you. You are powerful and mighty.
You conquered death in your earthly body,
and you conquered death for me. Amen.

---

10 Center for the Study of Citizenship, Wayne State University, http://www.clas.wayne.edu/Citizenship/Definition-of-Citizenship.

Here and There

Praise be to the God and Father of our Lord Jesus Christ! In his great mercy he has given us new birth into a living hope through the resurrection of Jesus Christ from the dead, and into an inheritance that can never perish, spoil or fade. This inheritance is kept in heaven for you, who through faith are shielded by God's power until the coming of the salvation that is ready to be revealed in the last time.

1 Peter 1:3–5 niv

Our faith in Jesus includes a "here and now" aspect as well as a "there and not yet" aspect. Here and now, we are made new because of Jesus and our faith in him. We have hope and joy that no one can take from us.

We also have an inheritance waiting for us in heaven. It is "there and not yet." This will be revealed to us in the future in heaven. God has given us this living hope in Jesus Christ. How blessed we are!

Reflect

Consider how your faith has changed you as a person. Identify what you can look forward to in heaven because of your belief in Jesus.

Thank you for the inheritance you have set forth for me, Lord. Thank you for your faithfulness today and always. Amen.

Walls of Protection

A man without self-control is like a city broken into
and left without walls.

PROVERBS 25:28 ESV

The Greek word for "self-control" is *egkrateia,* meaning,
"restraining passions and appetites." The opposite of self-
control is *akrasia*, which means, "excess, self-indulgence."[11]
Our culture praises excess and self-indulgence. These vices
are celebrated and glamorized as a mark of true success.

Our Proverb for today, however, tells us that self-control
is like a wall of protection around us. It protects us from the
enemy, who will use a lack of self-control against us to cross
our boundaries and attack us from within. That's why God
calls us to restrain our passions and appetites and cling to
what is good, holy, and pleasing.

Reflect

Imagine your self-control as a set of walls standing tall
and protecting your soul.

*Lord, thank you for your Word. You give me wisdom and the
keys to an abundant life. My heart's desire is to cling to you.
Amen.*

---

11   Strong, *Strong's Expanded Exhaustive Concordance of the
Bible*, #1466.

Mere Mortals

When I look at the night sky and see the work of your
fingers—the moon and the stars you set in place—what are
mere mortals that you should think about them, human
beings that you should care for them?

PSALM 8:3–4 NLT

When we shift our perspective from our life and the
problems that the day presents and focus instead on God
and his greatness, the moon and the stars that he hung in
our sky, the world falls into place. It might make us feel
small, or perhaps it's overwhelming to consider the gravity of
his love and care for us.

God knows us and loves us deeply and wholly. He
exists outside of the constraints of our world. He is powerful
and vast, and he pursues us. Our hearts should shine with
adoration, for we have been lost and are now found by the
King of kings.

Reflect

Sing a song of worship to Jesus today.
Praise him and how great and powerful he is.

*Lord, you are so good. Thank you for the beauty of this earth
and all your creation. There is so much beauty all around me,
and I am humbled that you know me so intimately.
You are my heart's desire, Lord. Amen.*

Hall of Faith

These people all died having faith in God. They did not receive what God had promised to them. But they could see far ahead to all the things God promised and they were glad for them. They knew they were strangers here. This earth was not their home.

HEBREWS 11:13 NLV

Our verse today is from the "hall of faith" chapter from Hebrews. Paul is listing off the faith titans of our heritage, and I love the point he makes here. Many of our role models in Jesus didn't see God's promises come to fruition, yet they persisted in their faith and knew God was good.

God always keeps his promises, yet he is primarily concerned with our hearts. He wants to be our soul's pure delight. He is true to his word and will fulfill his promises, but we love and worship him for who he is, not what he can do for us. Timing is his creation, and he is never late.

Reflect

What are some things you are waiting on from God?
How might you feel if you never receive them?
Talk to God about that today.

You are my prize, Lord. You are my soul's desire. Amen.

Bridegroom

No one hates his own body but feeds and cares for it, just as Christ cares for the church. And we are members of his body. As the Scriptures say, "A man leaves his father and mother and is joined to his wife, and the two are united into one." This is a great mystery, but it is an illustration of the way Christ and the church are one.

EPHESIANS 5:29–32 NLT

Jesus loves his church, but our church today has become divided. We should be known for the things we have in common, not the things that separate us. I am a mother of three boys, and it hurts my heart when they put each other down. Imagine how Jesus feels seeing his church at war within itself.

We are called to build up Christ's church. To love. Encourage. The church is his bride, and we should always honor and respect his bride—and our fellow brothers and sisters in Christ.

Reflect

How are you helping to strengthen Jesus' bride, the church? Pray for your pastor, invite a friend to Sunday service, or volunteer. Commit to doing something today.

Lord, help me to love your church. Open my eyes so I can see the ways I can make it strong for your glory. Amen.

Bring Honor

With this hope you can be happy even if you need to have sorrow and all kinds of tests for awhile. These tests have come to prove your faith and to show that it is good. Gold, which can be destroyed, is tested by fire. Your faith is worth much more than gold and it must be tested also. Then your faith will bring thanks and shining-greatness and honor to Jesus Christ when He comes again.

1 PETER 1:6–7 NLV

We can have joy even when we have trouble because of our faith in Jesus. Yes, we will have sorrow, but we are rooted in Jesus, and the waves of this world cannot shake the foundation of our faith.

What a humbling thought that our faith would provide honor to Jesus. What a privilege that is. We can choose to buy into the dramas of this world, or we can remain focused on Jesus. As we reach for him, he will always reach out to us.

Reflect

How can you bring Christ honor today?

Lord, I don't love the trials, but my hope is always in you. Thank you for being my constant. Amen.

Written in Heaven

"I have given you authority to trample on snakes and scorpions and to overcome all the power of the enemy; nothing will harm you. However, do not rejoice that the spirits submit to you, but rejoice that your names are written in heaven."

LUKE 10:19–20 NIV

We know the world has darkness to it. However, we have authority over that darkness in the name of Jesus. If we become aware of how much power we hold with the Holy Spirit, most of us would live dramatically different lives. Jesus Christ wins in the end, so we can live with boldness because we are guaranteed victory.

Jesus tells us that our names are written in heaven, in the Lamb's book of life (see Revelation 21:27). What a wondrous thought. We will exit this world and enter into another kingdom. Death will lose its sting, for we will live forever. Through God's grace, we enter into his glory.

Reflect

Consider how you would play a game differently if you knew your team would win. The same is true with our life. Walk in that confidence today.

Lord, thank you for giving me authority and power on earth. I submit to your will for my life. Amen.

Divine Encounters

When Elizabeth heard Mary's greeting, the baby leaped in her womb, and Elizabeth was filled with the Holy Spirit.

LUKE 1:41 NIV

Mary and Elizabeth were both pregnant, and even in the womb, Jesus' power was evident. Elizabeth's baby leaped for joy. Divine encounters like this can change our life. They change our perspective and our identity. Our whole life can shift in a moment because we encounter Jesus. Our life can also change slowly over time. God works in all ways. But an encounter from the Lord always demands a response. Does your faith cause you to leap?

Many times, when we feel like God is working the least in our life, he is actually working the most. He operates in the spiritual, and that precedes the physical. There were four hundred years of silence from God before Jesus entered the world. No prophets, no kings. Silence. We know now that God was working behind the scenes. He's still working today.

Reflect

Make space to encounter God today and prepare your soul to leap in his presence.

Lord, thank you for working in my life, behind the scenes. You cause my Spirit to leap. Amen.

October

Whatever You Have

Peter said, "I do not have silver and gold, but what I do have I give to you: In the name of Jesus Christ the Nazarene, walk!" And grasping him by the right hand, he raised him up; and immediately his feet and his ankles were strengthened.

ACTS 3:6–7 NASB

I want us to think about both of the people in this story. First, we have the crippled man. He is asking for pennies when he could be asking for new legs. In life, we tend to settle. We must remind ourselves of who we really are. God has placed us higher than angels! We have the weight of glory on us.

Let's shift our focus to Peter's response to the man: "What I do have I give to you." I love the posture of his heart. It reminds me of the Christmas song "Little Drummer Boy," where all the child has is a rhythm to play for Jesus, but he plays his best for Christ. Whatever you have is more than enough for God to use.

Reflect

Use what you have today for God's glory.

Jesus, I am yours. Amen.

God Waits for You

> The LORD must wait for you to come to him so he can show you his love and compassion. For the LORD is a faithful God. Blessed are those who wait for his help.
>
> ISAIAH 30:18 NLT

What a wild thought: the Lord waits for you. Have you ever waited for somebody? It can be frustrating. Yet God uses that opportunity to show us his love and compassion when we do show up for him. He isn't frustrated or bent out of shape. God graciously waits on us. He is patient and loving. He has a plan for us and wants to invite us into his will with our life, but he isn't pushy. He waits.

We will be blessed as we wait for God. That is a promise. We know God is faithful and understands waiting. He knows and understands what we are going through. He is the God of timing, and he is in control.

Reflect

Expect, look, and long for God today.

Lord, I wait on you for help. I trust your plan and your way. Thank you for being patient with me. Help me to be patient with others. Amen.

The Lord Laughs

The kings of the earth rise up and the rulers band together against the LORD and against his anointed, saying, "Let us break their chains and throw off their shackles." The One enthroned in heaven laughs; the Lord scoffs at them.

PSALM 2:2–4 NIV

This psalm is comforting during this time in history that we currently live in. Sometimes we must remind ourselves who is in control: God. Nothing surprises him. People who have true power have it from God.

We don't understand many things on this side of heaven, but we are called to have faith. The only way to have freedom is through Jesus. We can try to break chains on our own accord and strength, but God laughs at us. We have to learn to laugh with God. God will always be victorious. He has the world figured out and under his authority.

Reflect

Try to laugh with God today at the craziness of this world. Put your faith in him that he is in control.

Lord, you are the ruler of the world and my life.
You are enthroned in heaven, and I submit
to your glory and honor, Jesus. Amen.

Powerless Turned Powerful

God chose the foolish things of the world to shame the wise;
God chose the weak things of the world to shame the strong.

1 Corinthians 1:27 NIV

If you feel powerless in certain areas of your life, then you are in the perfect position. The Bible is full of stories of God using hopeless situations and weak people to demonstrate his power and presence. He shines through the holes of our weakness. Place yourself in a position of surrender and allow God to show up. We are powerless, but he is a mighty God. We are weak, but he is strong.

I was scrolling through Instagram yesterday, and I came across this account of people being kind, just videos of simple, kind gestures. It moved me to tears. Each video has millions of views. A simple gesture of love is powerful. Love is the greatest transformative source we have.

Reflect

Think of an area in your life that you feel powerless over.
Ask God to reveal himself and his plan to you.

Lord, I am weak and foolish compared to your great and mighty way. Use me to shine your glory on earth. Amen.

It Is Day

As long as it is day, we must do the works of him who sent me. Night is coming, when no one can work.

JOHN 9:4 NIV

I love the reminder of our verse today. Jesus knows that he has come to complete certain tasks that God has laid before him. The same is true with us and our lives. We have spiritual and natural "work" to do. He isn't saying we have to earn anything (love, heaven, etc.) by completing tasks. However, Jesus has a sense of urgency because of his relationship with the Father. I want to serve my children and get things done for them not because I want to earn their respect but out of my love for them.

The "night" Jesus is referring to here is death. None of us is getting out of here alive, and while you are on God's green earth, you have work to do, work designed specifically for you and your talents. What an honor!

Reflect

Identify what work you feel God has for you to do today. Do it!

Jesus, thank you for creating me.
I want my life to honor you. Amen.

Unshakable Hope

Command those who are rich in this present world not to be arrogant nor to put their hope in wealth, which is so uncertain, but to put their hope in God, who richly provides us with everything for our enjoyment.

1 Timothy 6:17 niv

What are you hoping for? We can hope that our team makes the playoffs or our kid gets the right teacher or a certain boy asks us out. The world always offers ways to put our hope into earthly things. Our verse today reminds us to put our hope in Jesus.

Hope is a favorable and confident expectation. What are you expecting God to do in your life? He will richly provide for you and give you a life that is enjoyable, as our verse proclaims today. When our hope is in God, it becomes unshakable. Nothing can steal us from our hope in Christ.

Reflect

What are you expecting God to do in your life right now? Tell him.

Jesus, my hope is in you. Guide me in all I do. Show me your way. Amen.

Prisoner of the Lord

As a prisoner for the Lord, then, I urge you to live a life
worthy of the calling you have received.

EPHESIANS 4:1 NIV

Being a prisoner of the Lord releases us from every other
prison. Depression, anxiety, addiction, loneliness, the list is
never-ending of the bondage we can find ourselves shackled
to. Jesus offers us a life of freedom when we intentionally
surrender to him.

Do you know the calling you have in Christ? We are
called more than conquerors (Romans 8:37). We live from
glory to glory (2 Corinthians 3:18). We are heirs to the King
of kings (Romans 8:17). Many times, we have the mindset of
a captive and use words and thoughts of weakness. We are
called higher! We have a calling on our life because of Jesus,
and that calling is magnificent.

Reflect

Are you living a life worthy of the calling you have in Jesus?
Claim the life you are called to live.

*Lord, I am your prisoner. I am set free from every other
stronghold in Jesus' name. Amen.*

Talking Donkey

The donkey said to Balaam, "Am I not your own donkey,
which you have always ridden, to this day? Have I been in
the habit of doing this to you?"
"No," he said.

NUMBERS 22:30 NIV

Did God use a talking donkey? Absolutely. God can do anything and use anything. He used words and spoke the earth into existence. He used a fish to put Jonah on the right path. He uses marriage to demonstrate to us how much Jesus loves his bride, the church. He uses our weakness to showcase his strength.

God has no limitations and invites us into a life of faith and freedom, but he asks us to surrender. Our God can do anything. A talking donkey isn't that wild of a story when we look at all the wondrous miracles that fill the Bible.

Reflect

Do you believe nothing is impossible for God?
Talk to him about that today.

*Lord, your Word is filled with the impossible, and I believe
every story. You are capable of more than anything I can
imagine. Thank you for being a big God. Amen.*

Spirit of Power

God has not given us a spirit of fear and timidity,
but of power, love, and self-discipline.

2 TIMOTHY 1:7 NLT

The idea that Paul encourages us to remember we were not
given a spirit of fear highlights the fact that there is a spirit
of fear. It isn't hard to recognize that the spirit of fear is a real
thing. Just look around our world. People are living in fear.
Fear of the unknown, fear of death, fear of the future.

God doesn't want us to live in fear. He gives us his Spirit,
which is of power, love, and self-discipline. We are called
to be bold. We are called to live with God's powerful spirit
inside of us. Let's be mindful to not allow the Spirit of fear to
control our thoughts.

Reflect

Live today mindful of the type of Spirit God has entrusted
you with. Call out the spirit of fear when you feel thoughts
of fear creep into your mind.

*Lord, thank you for your Holy Spirit. Thank you for the seal
you place on me and the plans you have for my life.
I love you. Amen.*

Encourage

Encourage each other and build each other up,
just as you are already doing.
1 THESSALONIANS 5:11 NLT

When we encourage others, we often renew their confidence
and even bring them hope. I love this idea of giving hope.
We show people Jesus. We guide those around us to set
their eyes on the Lord. When we choose to see our life and
the things unfolding around us through the lens of eternity,
hope always transcends.

Who in your life builds you up? Would someone think
of you when asked the same question? We get to help,
stimulate, support, and give advice, courage, and vision to
those God places in front of us. When we shift our actions,
wanting to encourage and build up those around us, we offer
grace in their small shortcomings.

Reflect

Build up at least two people today. Let the first person
be a stranger and the second a dear friend.

*Lord, I worship you. Place people in my life whom you want
me to encourage today. Give me words to speak life over them.
Amen.*

Wisdom and Kindness

She opens her mouth with wisdom,
and on her tongue is the law of kindness.

PROVERBS 31:26 NKJV

Proverbs 31 describes a virtuous woman we can all look up to. I love the idea that she "opens her mouth." I myself am opinionated and not afraid to open my mouth and share my point of view. This idea that she speaks wisdom and isn't afraid to speak up brings me encouragement. It is equally important to note that she speaks wisdom with kindness. Many times we fall one way or the other. Too outspoken or too much of a pushover.

Let's be mindful to always speak wisdom with kindness. We are called to and capable of both.

Reflect

Speak up today with the wisdom God has given you!
Our culture, now more than ever, needs women
who speak truth in kindness.

Lord, I pray you will give me wisdom.
Give me the courage to speak boldly, with kindness,
and with an overflowing of love. Amen.

Soft Answer

A soft answer turns away wrath,
but a harsh word stirs up anger.

PROVERBS 15:1 NKJV

When we injure someone or there is conflict in our life, we should always try to resolve the situation. If you want others to receive your message well, say it the way you would want to hear it. Being harsh never serves anyone well, especially since we are called to be ambassadors of Jesus. We can offer our point of view in a gentle manner.

"Patience can persuade a prince, and soft speech can break bones," as Proverbs 25:15 (NLT) tells us. Comparing these two Proverbs shows us that our words can stir up anger or turn it down. Let's choose soft answers and soft speech.

Reflect

Practice the way you say things today.
Invite a spirit of grace into your presence.

Lord, always give me soft words, especially in the middle of heated conversations. I bow down to you. Reveal any pride in me and let me submit it to you, Jesus. Amen.

Multiplied

May mercy, peace,
and love be multiplied to you.

JUDE 1:2 ESV

When everything seems to be falling apart, we must remember that God is working it out behind the scenes. May our focus today, and always, be on Jesus. Even if the winds are strong and the storm is booming, if we focus on Jesus, we can walk on water. Our life can showcase God's power and love when we are filled with his Holy Spirit.

The idea of mercy, peace, and love multiplying in us is a beautiful thought. As we walk closely with God, mercy, peace, and love increase greatly in us.

Reflect

Choose to rest and not stress today. Spend time today thinking about God's mercy, peace, and love.

Lord, I claim the promises of this verse over myself today. Let your mercy, peace, and love be multiplied in me. Through my words, thoughts, and actions, let these blessings prevail.

Refiner's Fire

"I have refined you, though not as silver;
I have tested you in the furnace of affliction."
ISAIAH 48:10 NIV

God has refined you and continues to refine you. We want life to be easy, and we pray for the path with the least pain. But God can use affliction to make us holy and our faith strong. It is never fun and can be quite painful when you are in the "furnace of affliction." However, God always walks with us through the hardships of our life. Even when we feel alone or full of doubt, God never leaves or forsakes us.

Remember that gratefulness comes when our hearts are full, not when our hands are full. The process of refinement will lead you to the promises of your life. We must surrender and trust the Lord. We can be grateful even in the midst of God's refining fire.

Reflect

Allow God's refining fire to have its way with you and
do the work he intends to do. Focus on him today
with an intentional, grateful spirit.

Lord, I trust you. I love you and know that you love me. Amen.

Strength and Dignity

She is clothed with strength and dignity;
she can laugh at the days to come.

PROVERBS 31:25 NIV

How can this woman laugh at the days to come? She is filled with the hope of her faith. When we are focused on God and his promises, we are filled with hope and peace. We know the plans God has for us are good. We know that he who made his promises is faithful. Jesus tells us, "Everything is possible for one who believes" (Mark 9:23 NIV), so how can we not be full of hope?

The imagery of being clothed in strength and dignity is quite powerful. As women, we want to be clothed in jewelry or a beautiful garment, but this promise offers us so much more. Strength and dignity. Picture yourself today wrapped in God's strength and dignity.

Reflect

Have peace and joy in the present adventure.
Set your mind on hope.

Lord, my hope is in you. Thank you for wrapping me in strength, Jesus. I have dignity because I belong to you. Thank you, Father. Amen.

Seek God

Those who know your name trust in you, for you, LORD,
have never forsaken those who seek you.

PSALM 9:10 NIV

Do you trust the Lord? Have you felt abandoned by God in the past? This promise tells us that God will never forsake those who know him. If we seek God, we will know God and experience his faithfulness. Do you know God intimately?

As we spend time with God, reading his Word and worshiping his presence, we taste and see that he is good and faithful. Even when our situation remains the same, our hope is renewed because we trust in the Lord. As we seek God, we will find him. Oh, how sweet a promise!

Reflect

Reflect today on different seasons of your life.
Good times and bad. Are you seeking
God in your life through these times? How?

God, you will not abandon those who search for you.
I claim this promise today and praise you, Lord!
You are a good God, and I worship who you are. Amen.

Christ in Me

God is within her, she will not fall;
God will help her at break of day.

PSALM 46:5 NIV

God is within you. You can't fail. Our Scripture verse reminds us today that we are filled with the precious and powerful Holy Spirit of God. We will fall and move through seasons of darkness, but God is always there to rescue us.

Our minds can run away with fear and doubt. It is our duty to combat the lies with truth. As we rest on the truths and promises of God, we step into power and freedom. God promises us freedom, but we have to choose it for ourselves. God is within you, sweet girl! You can't fail.

Reflect

Remind yourself throughout the day that Christ is within you. You can't fail. Repeat and claim this for yourself today.

Jesus, you are within me, and I can't fail with you.
You will help me and guide me. I claim this over my life today.
I thank you for your love and goodness.
I worship your holy name. Amen.

Live Freely

"Keep company with me and you'll learn
to live freely and lightly."
MATTHEW 11:28–30 MSG

God invites us to a life of freedom, light, and rest. We find REST by Releasing Every Sabotaging Thought. As we spend time with the Lord, we become rooted in the truth. The more we know the truth, the better we become at recognizing lies, and the more we can release them.

We can stand against the destructive thoughts with the truth of the gospel. We were made for a victorious life. We are not supposed to live feeling defeated, ashamed, or condemned. Claim a life that is free and light.

Reflect

Share this verse with at least two people today. Text a friend or tell a stranger at the checkout line. God will put people in your life today who need reminding of this truth.

*Lord, I desire to live the life you have created me for.
I invite you into all the pieces of me. I love you. Amen.*

A Chosen Generation

You are a chosen generation, a royal priesthood, a holy
nation, His own special people, that you may proclaim the
praises of Him who called you out of darkness
into His marvelous light.

1 PETER 2:9 NKJV

Our prayer today is that we would be rooted in the reality of
God's truth. You are chosen and special. You were made to
walk in safety and security. You were created to shine your true
self, which gives God glory since you are made in his image.

Many of us feel ashamed or condemned or broken. We
believe so many lies. God made us to walk righteously. The
Bible tells us that God goes before, behind, above, and below
us. We should proclaim his goodness to all we meet, but in
order to do that, we must experience freedom in our own
lives. Rest in God's truth and know who you are today, sweet
sister. You are royalty.

Reflect

Pay attention to the thoughts you think about yourself today.

*I praise your holy name, Lord. You have called me
out of darkness, and I worship you. Amen.*

Altogether Beautiful

You are altogether beautiful, my darling;
there is no flaw in you.
SONG OF SONGS 4:7 NIV

God created you in his image. You are beautiful. God's Spirit shines through you. *Altogether* means completely, totally. I love the idea that we are created completely and totally beautiful. Society often teaches that parts of us are prettier than other parts and that we need products and procedures to be beautiful. What a lie. All of us, every part, is created in the image of God and altogether beautiful.

May heaven be glorified like never before because we possess the confidence to know who we are, the beauty of God that is magnified through us. May we bring God glory and honor because of our confidence in what he created us to be. There is no shame or condemnation in Christ! Let's boldly walk in the truth of the beauty we possess.

Reflect

Be confident today in your thoughts about yourself.
Speak beauty over yourself today.

Lord, thank you for creating me altogether beautiful.
I pray to walk in the confidence of who
you made me to be. Amen.

Let Another

Let another praise you, and not your own mouth;
a stranger, and not your own lips.

PROVERBS 27:2 ESV

"Enough about me; what do you think about me?" was a saying I grew up with. My mom would often say it to my brothers and me if we were talking about ourselves too much. We have to keep our egos in check, a heart check, that only we can give ourselves.

Our culture praises an Instagram flex or even a seductive post, but no one likes a bragger or a boaster. They are simply not fun to be around. Most importantly, the Lord loves humility, and remaining humble is a great practice. When we spend time with Jesus, our hearts tend to fall into place, and we seek to give him glory, not ourselves. Success in any form comes from God's favor. Let the praises that come from our mouths always be for the King of kings. Of course we should encourage those around us, but let's remain humble in our hearts.

Reflect

Pay attention to the words you speak today. No bragging.

Lord, all I have is because of you.
I praise you, Jesus. Amen.

Hovering

> The earth was without form and void, and darkness
> was over the face of the deep. And the Spirit of God
> was hovering over the face of the waters.
>
> GENESIS 1:2 ESV

"Spirit of God" comes from the Hebrew phrase *ruach elohim*, which has been interpreted as a "great wind."[12] This is important because as Christians, we believe that God created everything out of nothing and is omnipotent.

This verse describes God at the beginning of the world. The same Holy Spirit that formed the universe is alive and resides within us today. The powerful, loving, mighty Spirit of God made our bodies its temple when we accepted Jesus as our Savior.

Reflect

Listen to the song "Rest on Us" by Maverick City Music
Hall. Listen to the words and worship the
Spirit of the living God today.

Lord, fill me with your Holy Spirit.
You are here, and I know you are moving.
I trust you and worship you. Amen.

---

12   Dan Clenendin, "The 'Great Wind of God,'" *Journey with Jesus*
(website).

Christ Is All

Here there is no Gentile or Jew, circumcised or
uncircumcised, barbarian, Scythian, slave or free,
but Christ is all, and is in all.

COLOSSIANS 3:11 NIV

This verse comes at the end of Paul's thoughts about a life full
of holy living. He is encouraging us to focus on the things of
eternity and to set our minds on the lovely, not the negative.
Division is from the devil. Although it may be difficult to
love people when you disagree with them, we must focus on
what we share in common with them, not what separates us.

Of course this is a delicate line to walk. We always stand
up for truth and convictions in our heart, but we do this out
of love. We treat everyone as God sees them: loved.

Reflect

With every conversation and encounter you have with
others today, remember that Christ is in those people too.
Treat them as dearly loved as they are by our Father.

*Lord, you are my everything. I want to love as you love.
I want to decrease and have you increase in my life. Amen.*

Hope and Encouragement

May our Lord Jesus Christ himself and God our Father, who loved us and by his grace gave us eternal encouragement and good hope, encourage your hearts and strengthen you in every good deed and word.

2 Thessalonians 2:16–17 NIV

We have eternal encouragement and hope in Jesus. We strengthen our faith with every good deed and good word we say. That is on the table for us, and all we have to do is claim it for ourselves and our lives.

I know a lot of believers who are living defeated lives. I know a lot of women who feel they have lost their hope. We read in today's verse that through God's grace, we have eternal hope and encouragement. One of the best things about grace is that you can't lose it. It isn't earned, and it can't be lost.

Reflect

Let us remember today the hope and eternal encouragement we have in Jesus. Remind yourself and your loved ones around you of God's goodness, faithfulness, mercy, and love.

Lord, I pray the same prayer Saint Paul prayed many years ago. Encourage my heart, Jesus, and strengthen me in every deed and word. Amen.

Close Watch

Keep a close watch on yourself and on the teaching.
Persist in this, for by so doing you will save
both yourself and your hearers.

1 Timothy 4:16 esv

My kids have my mannerisms. I didn't teach them how
to move their hands like me or walk like me, but they
do. They watch me without even knowing it and act how
I act. Whom are you watching without even knowing
it? Whose mannerisms are you picking up, maybe even
unintentionally?

As we spend time with Jesus, we start acting like him
and talking like him. Our hearts start to mold into his heart.
We believe in a living God who is worthy of our devotion.
Let's live in a region of faith, bold faith, in an ever-present
God. Let's have our lives reflect what our hearts hold true.

Reflect

Keep a close watch on yourself as our verse reminds us
today. Think about who is "teaching" you. Not just from the
pulpit on Sundays but also on your phone and
in your friend group.

Lord, let me always lead people to you.
I pray my faith will encourage those around me. Amen.

Devote Yourself

Devote yourselves to prayer,
being watchful and thankful.
COLOSSIANS 4:2 NIV

What a powerful verse! The word *devote* means "to give over or direct (time, money, effort, etc.) to a cause, enterprise, or activity." We are encouraged to "give over" our time and resources to prayer.

The second part of this verse is particularly insightful. Prayer includes being watchful and thankful. Do you spend time thanking God for your blessings? Do you ask God to open your eyes to see his handiwork all around you? Are you waiting in hope on the Lord right now in your life? God deserves our devotion, including our prayers.

Reflect

Make a list of what you are devoted to. Be honest by thinking about how you spend your time, thoughts, and money. Be sure to add prayer to this list.

Lord, I thank you for my life and the blessings you bestow on me. I see you working all around me, and your presence makes my heart sing. I rest in you, Jesus. Amen.

Scripture

All Scripture is breathed out by God and profitable for
teaching, for reproof, for correction, and for training
in righteousness.

2 TIMOTHY 3:16 ESV

This is a very important verse for us believers today. All
Scripture is "breathed out by God." The Word of God is from
the Holy Spirit. Many people try to misuse or twist God's
Word, but the Word of the Lord is eternal.

God's Word is holy, living, active, powerful, and true.
God cannot lie, for that is not his character. As we read God's
Word, our faith increases. We can read the same verse a
thousand times, and every time God will reveal something
new or speak to us in a fresh way. When speaking to a friend,
a verse might pop into our minds to share. These moments
are the workings of the Holy Spirit.

Reflect

This verse tells us that we must read God's Word to train
in righteousness. Ask God to increase your desire to be
righteous. Spend time reading God's Word today.

*Lord, thank you for the gift of Scripture. I pray you will
speak to me today. Meet with me as I carve out time
to meet with you. Amen.*

Take Up Your Cross

[Jesus] said to all, "If anyone would come after me, let him deny himself and take up his cross daily and follow me."

LUKE 9:23 ESV

Jesus is asking three things of us, his followers, here. The first is to deny ourselves. This doesn't mean that Jesus wants us to live a sad and lonely life. He desires for us to pursue our hopes and dreams. However, he is telling us that we will have to say no to our fleshly desires. Our culture likes to tell us to "follow our heart," but that is a lie. Our heart will tell us to give up, not apologize, and not forgive. Follow Jesus. Follow Scripture.

The second point is that every single day we must decide whom we will serve. Will we serve ourselves and our desires, or will we put Jesus first? The third point is to follow God. Many of us follow ourselves and then ask God to bless our decisions. Allow him to lead and see where he takes you.

Reflect

Take up your cross and go after Jesus today, whatever and however that looks for you in your life.

Jesus, I am yours. Amen.

The Lord's Hand

The hand of the Lord was with them,
and a great number who believed turned to the Lord.

ACTS 11:21 ESV

God has more to say to you than you have to say to him.
Often, I feel him encouraging me to be still in his presence.
To wait for him to move and perform miracles in my life.
I want to see miracles in my life, and a miracle is anything
God can do that I can't.

Our verse today tells us that many believed and turned
to the Lord because the hand of God was with them. I
believe the hand of God is with us today. Believe it and claim
it for your life. Ask God for bold adventures to give him
glory that only could happen by his hand.

Reflect

Go through your day knowing that the Lord's hand is with
you. At the end of your day, reflect on how this awareness
changed you. Were you bolder? Did you feel safe?
Talk to God about it.

*Thank you, Jesus, for keeping your hand with me. I pray for
miracles. I pray for boldness and your favor. Amen.*

Grow Strong

> The child grew and became strong; he was filled with
> wisdom, and the grace of God was on him.
>
> LUKE 2:40 NIV

Little is known about Jesus during his formative years, but this verse offers us insight. It's also a great prayer to pray over ourselves and the people in our life. I, too, want to grow strong in the Lord. I desire his grace to cover me and his wisdom to fill me. I want to be spiritually mature. Spiritual maturity is a longing to hear God's voice.

What good is the promised land without the promiser himself? What good is our salvation without our Savior? Jesus is our great reward. As we experience his presence in our lives, we can't go without it. Make it a habit to pray for an experience of God's presence for ourselves and our loved ones.

Reflect

Pray today's verse over the people God puts on your heart. Spend time picturing the words you speak becoming a reality in their lives.

Lord, I pray for my family and myself today. Let us grow and become strong, rooted in you, Jesus. Fill us with your wisdom and pour your grace on us, Lord. Amen.

Ask and Believe

They said to her, "You are out of your mind." But she kept insisting that it was so, and they kept saying, "It is his angel!"

ACTS 12:15 ESV

Our verse today requires a little context. Peter is in prison, and the disciples are all together and praying for him inside a house. It's safe to assume that they felt scared, discouraged, and sad. Their friend and leader was most likely going to die in jail. But Acts 12 goes on to detail the story of Peter's escape. An angel appeared and led him out of jail. Peter thought he was dreaming, but when he realized it was reality, he headed to his friends' home.

Peter knocked on the door, and a girl answered. She saw Peter and ran up to tell everyone. What did the disciples do? They exclaimed, "You are out of your mind!" But it was indeed Peter. Their prayers had been answered. When we ask God for something, be prepared for him to answer!

Reflect

Ask God for something bold today
and believe that he will answer you.

Lord, I want to ask and believe.
Help me with my unbelief. Amen.

November

Cleansed

Jesus asked, "Were not all ten cleansed?
Where are the other nine?"

LUKE 17:17 NIV

Our Scripture verse today comes from the Gospel of Luke.
You can read the whole story in Luke 17:11–17, but let me
sum it up for you. Jesus was on his way to Jerusalem when
ten men with leprosy saw him from a distance. They asked
Jesus to have pity on them. Jesus told them to go to their
priests, and on their way, each of them was healed!

One of the men decided to turn back and thank Jesus.
One out of ten. Be that one today, sweet sister. See God's
healing and activity all around you and give thanks.

Reflect

Thank Jesus today. Spend time in prayer or worship,
on a walk or in your room. However you choose
to give thanks today is for you to decide.

*Lord, I bow down at your feet. You have healed me.
You have saved me. You have blessed me.
I am so thankful for your goodness in my life. Amen.*

More Love

"By this all people will know that you are my disciples, if you have love for one another."

JOHN 13:35 ESV

People will know of our faith in Jesus by how well we love. We will not be known as believers for our careers, our politics, or our social status. We will be known by our love.

There is so much division around us today, and the world needs more love. Love drives out fear. Love is eternal and covers a multitude of sins. Love never fails. Love is the greatest and strongest force in this world. God is love, and as we spend time with him, we begin to act like him.

Reflect

Go above and beyond to love everyone God puts in your path today. Be mindful of anyone God puts on your heart and love them in a special way.

Jesus, you are the lover of my soul. You are my King, and I can love others because of the love I experience through you. Thank you for loving me. Amen.

Focus

Finally, brothers and sisters, whatever is true, whatever is noble, whatever is right, whatever is pure, whatever is lovely, whatever is admirable—if anything is excellent or praiseworthy—think about such things.

PHILIPPIANS 4:8 NIV

I find my mind grows anxious when I focus on things outside of my control. The to-do list, the stressors, and the everyday drama of my day will always be present. And when I allow my mind to constantly focus on the negative, then my state of mind is full of fear.

As I shift my focus toward Jesus and meditate on all the good that surrounds me, on God's glory in creation, on all the blessings of my day, the frequency at which I'm operating shifts to a higher level.

Reflect

Be mindful of your thoughts today. Focus on what is true, noble, right, and lovely today. Let your words be uplifting and your posture admirable. Not out of duty but out of awe for Jesus.

Lord, I set my mind on things eternal. My soul is eternal, and I desire my thoughts to be pure. Amen.

Unceasing

The steadfast love of the LORD never ceases; his mercies never come to an end; they are new every morning; great is your faithfulness. "The LORD is my portion," says my soul, "therefore I will hope in him."

LAMENTATIONS 3:22–24 ESV

Read this verse again. I'm not sure if you need to be reminded of God's steadfast love today, or perhaps you can just keep it tucked away in your heart. The good news is eternal. We place our hope in the Lord. He is faithful, loving, and rich in mercies.

Another word for *steadfast* is *unwavering*. God's love for you not only never ceases, but it is also firm and never wavers. Anyone who seeks God will find him. Everyone is spiritual, and if they seek God with their heart, then they will encounter his unwavering love.

Reflect

Think about the idea of your soul declaring, "The Lord is my portion." What does that mean to you? Talk to God about that.

Lord, thank you for your steadfast love. I praise you for your faithfulness to me and your mercy. Amen.

Pray and Persist

Jesus told his disciples a parable to show them that they should always pray and not give up.

LUKE 18:1 NIV

The Holy Spirit wants to meet us in our prayer time. When we read God's Word, it transforms our minds. God gives us wisdom and can help our unbelief. We have permission to encounter God and pray bold prayers. We can do powerful things with our lives if we align our hearts to God's will.

Jesus is encouraging us to pray. He wants us to keep asking God for our dream or healing and to not give up. God delights in us and wants to make our dreams a reality, bigger than we could ever imagine. That is what his Word tells us. Many believers have settled into dry, quiet times and small prayers. Don't give up and always pray, like Jesus tells us.

Reflect

What is God urging you to pray about today?
What is he pushing you to not give up on?

*Lord, I want to have a bold prayer life. I want to know you and your Spirit in a real and powerful way.
Transform my thoughts and my mindset. Amen.*

Our Inheritance

They shall have no inheritance among their fellow Israelites;
the LORD is their inheritance, as he promised them.

DEUTERONOMY 18:2 NIV

God can call us to anything and use us in any situation.
Nothing is beneath us. We must be willing to follow him
because he is our inheritance. He is our promised land.
Partial obedience is still disobedience. Our lives must be
completely surrendered to the King of kings.

The disciples are a great example of dedication. We read
how many times they didn't fully understand Jesus, but still
they trusted him. They followed him with all they had. We
can't give our lives partially or in pieces. We give it all to Jesus.

Reflect

Are you all in for God? Think about the things, tangible and
intangible, that you hold on to tightly in your life right now.
Spend time today surrendering those areas to God.

*Lord, you are my great reward. You are my promise,
my Savior, and my King. I want more of you, Father.
I want to fall more in love with you. Amen.*

See God

She called, "Samson, the Philistines are upon you!" He awoke
  from his sleep and thought, "I'll go out as before and shake
  myself free." But he did not know that the LORD had left him.

JUDGES 16:20 NIV

Our verse today is about Samson, arguably the most famous
of the judges from the Old Testament. All the judges were
declared to have the hand of God on them, but the book of
Judges declares not once but three times (14:6, 19; 15:14)
that God's hand was on Samson. However, Samson gave in
to his sinful desires, and God departed from him. Samson
didn't even notice.

Luckily for us, we live in the New Testament era, where
the Holy Spirit cannot leave us once we have accepted Jesus
as our Lord and Savior. We need to know God above all else.
You have a seal on you, and you belong to God. We can,
however, miss the presence of God. Be mindful to see God
working all around you today.

Reflect

Turn your eyes to see God all around you today.

Lord, open the eyes of my heart.
Help me see you. Amen.

Fresh Authority

A little sleep, a little slumber, a little folding of the hands to
rest—and poverty will come on you like a thief
and scarcity like an armed man.

PROVERBS 6:10–11 NIV

This verse is not saying that you have to work, work, work to
find success in the eyes of the Lord. God created the world
in six days, and then he rested. God loves seasons of rest.
However, our human nature has a tendency to let excuses or
laziness rob us of our purpose.

We need a fresh authority to finish what God has started
in us. Don't believe the lies or self-doubt that enter your
mind. God has called you to something, and you must do it.
You are the hands and feet of Jesus. You can do this, friend!

Reflect

What have you been procrastinating about that you felt
called to do? Honor God by finishing it.

Lord, I hand my life over to you. All my dreams and talents.
My work, my passions, and my relationships.
Use my life and resources for your glory. Amen.

Promised Land

Moses took the bones of Joseph with him, for he had placed
the children of Israel under solemn oath, saying, "God will
surely visit you, and you shall carry up my bones
from here with you."

EXODUS 13:19 NKJV

Moses and the Israelites took the bones of Joseph out of Egypt,
through the wilderness, and into the promised land. What a
beautiful image tucked away in Scripture. Joseph had gone
through his own wilderness, having been sold into slavery by
his brothers. He was then wrongly thrown into prison.

Yet Joseph never lost faith. He trusted that God would
bring him to the promised land. The words in Exodus give us
a glimpse into the shared oath that God and Joseph had. He
shares the same oath with you.

Reflect

Identify your promised land. Talk to God about it
and claim it in faith with your heavenly Father.

*Lord, I want to know you more. The more I learn about you,
the more I trust and love you. Thank you for being
a good and mighty God. Amen.*

Living as Jesus Did

Whoever claims to live in him must live as Jesus did.

1 JOHN 2:6 NIV

If we call ourselves Christians, we must live like Jesus lived. Jesus is victorious, and so are we. Jesus is powerful, and our lives are full of power. Jesus was bold, forgiving, nonjudgmental, loving, and looked at the hearts of people. We, too, should live that way. It's a tall order!

Many of us live with a watered-down, black-and-white version of what God has called us to step into. We are called to be the light of the world and heirs to the throne of the holy of holies. We must live like Jesus. Let us remember where our identity lies and whom we belong to and lead lives worthy of the calling that God has placed on our hearts.

Reflect

Choose one of the qualities mentioned in today's reflection and focus on showing it to others.

Jesus, I'm sorry for believing the lies and letting fear reign in certain areas of my life. My prayer is to lead a life like yours. Amen.

Angels

"Do you think I cannot call on my Father, and he will at once put at my disposal more than twelve legions of angels?"

MATTHEW 26:53 NIV

A "legion" would be a well-known word in Jesus' day. It is a military term referring to a group of about six thousand Roman soldiers. Jesus was saying that he could call on God, and in an instant, about seventy-two thousand angels would be by his side, ready to do as he commanded. Angels never die, so the same angels from Jesus' time are ready to answer our prayers today.

Let's live our life today aware of the power at our disposal through Jesus. We are here to do God's will, and though we can feel powerless at times, this is not our reality. God is powerful and wants to use his power through us to complete his will on earth. It is time to rise!

Reflect

Be bold today! Live in the reality that angels are at your side.

Lord, thank you for the power of your presence in my life. Your will, your way, God. Amen.

Matters of the Heart

He did not need any testimony about mankind,
for he knew what was in each person.

JOHN 2:25 NIV

Though short, this verse is powerful. The first thing we can lean into is that Jesus is always interested in our heart. He doesn't care what we say, what we do, or how we try to earn his love. He knows our motives and the core of who we are. As we invest in him, spend time with him, and soak up his Word, we fall more and more in love with him. As we give, serve, worship, and learn, we intertwine with Jesus.

The second point that stands out is that he knows us. Jesus doesn't need to get to know you because he already knows everything about you. He loves you. He made you. He is pursuing you. He has plans for you. Believe and receive that truth today.

Reflect

Take some time today to honestly examine your heart.
Are you investing in your relationship with God?

Lord, thank you for knowing me. Thank you for loving me so well. I give you today. Let me shine your light. Amen.

After God's Heart

"God removed Saul and replaced him with David, a man about whom God said, 'I have found David son of Jesse, a man after my own heart. He will do everything I want him to do.'"

ACTS 13:22 NLT

In this chapter of Acts, Paul gives the history of God saving Israel. David was an important figure and king in Israel's history. He was full of moral corruption, yet God declared David as a man after his heart. Yes, David was imperfect, but David sought God. Yes, David messed up many times, but God knew he could trust him because David belonged to God.

What is in the heart of God? Love, joy, peace, patience, kindness, gentleness, and goodness. We want to go after these things. We want to look for those things throughout our days and in every situation. Let's go after God's heart, for there we will find things of eternity.

Reflect

Think of how you are going after God's own heart in your life. Talk to God about that today.

Jesus, I desire you. I want my desires to align with your will over my life. Pour your favor on me, Jesus. Amen.

Everything in It

The God who made the world and everything in it, being Lord
of heaven and earth, does not live in temples made by man.

ACTS 17:24 ESV

God made the world and everything in it. Sometimes it feels
like things are out of control. We must remember that God
made everything, and mere men can't contain or even fully
understand him. We are created. He is the Creator. We place
our trust in his holy name because he is worthy, trustworthy,
good, and faithful.

His Word declares his glory, and our earth declares
his might. From a sunset and the pounding ocean waves to
the vast snow-capped mountains, look around and witness
creation proclaiming his majesty. Our phones and the media
seem to place fear and stress in our hearts, but if we look at
everything God has created, our hearts can be quieted. We
can find calmness and rest in God's grace.

Reflect

Try to look around more today at all God created.
He lives in you and me. Seek his presence today.

*Jesus, I praise your name for all you have created. Your glory
is all around me. Thank you for your beauty. Amen.*

Glory to Glory

We all, with unveiled face, beholding the glory of the Lord
are being transformed into the same image from
one degree of glory to another. For this comes from
the Lord who is the Spirit.

2 CORINTHIANS 3:18 ESV

We live in victory. We are called glory to glory. Increase
to increase. Start strong and finish strong. We shouldn't
care whether the things we are called to are unknown or
successful. We just need to be faithful to God's calling.

We tend to pray for comfort when we should pray for
character. God transforms who we are into his image. What
a beautiful calling he invites us to step into.

Reflect

Repeat this verse to yourself several times, text it to a friend,
or write it on a notecard. Meditate on what
God proclaims over you.

Jesus, thank you for your glory resting on me.
Thank you for victory and for living a life of love.
I want my life to be a living testimony of your goodness.
Pour your Spirit out on me. Amen.

Favor of God

Whatever I am now, it is all because God poured out his special favor on me—and not without results. For I have worked harder than any of the other apostles; yet it was not I but God who was working through me by his grace.

1 CORINTHIANS 15:10 NLT

Alexander Raleigh, a nineteenth century minister and author, defined grace as "the free and unmerited favour of God."[13] Do you walk in the truth that you have God's favor? You haven't earned it; in fact, your actions should be a response to his grace, not to *earn* his grace. Paul declares that he changed, and "whatever [he is] now" is all because of God's grace.

As believers, our lives should look different because of our hope and joy in Jesus. Our vision and reality become altered because we live in the freedom of God's love. God's grace is poured out on you today. He loves you and favors you. Believe that and live today responding to that beautiful truth.

Reflect

Spend time today considering the grace of God over you. Praise him for his grace.

Jesus, thank you for your grace and favor. I love you. I praise your holy name. Amen.

---

13   Alexander Raleigh, *Quiet Resting Places and Other Sermons* (Edinburgh: Adam and Charles Black, 1863), 145.

Men and Women

In the Lord woman is not independent of man, nor is man independent of woman. For as woman came from man, so also man is born of woman. But everything comes from God.

1 CORINTHIANS 11:11–12 NIV

Today's culture sometimes pits men and women against each other, which goes against God's Word. The reality is that men and women rely on each other. A woman can glorify God in ways a man cannot and vice versa. We were made to fit together, work together, and complement each other. Our verses for today stress that we should feel equal to one another. It's the way we are created.

We can read the Bible and disagree with what it says, but we are not God. When we start to think we know more than him, we walk into a lie that will wreak havoc on our lives.

Reflect

Think about how you complement, balance, and respect the men in your life.

Help me use my femininity to point others to you, Jesus. Amen.

Tithe and Offering

Moses said to the whole Israelite community, "This is what the LORD has commanded: From what you have, take an offering for the LORD. Everyone who is willing is to bring to the LORD an offering of gold, silver and bronze."

EXODUS 35:4–5 NIV

Tithing is the spiritual principle of giving God the first 10 percent of all we receive, showcasing that we know there is more to come. God doesn't want our leftovers. He wants our firstfruits. God has given us freedom to place our trust in him and give him our first as an act of obedience and faith.

It's easy to feel like we are working hard but not feeling blessed. The blessing comes from obedience. That is, you can't receive a blessing without obedience. Tithing is not just financial; it involves everything. We give God the first moments of our day, our talents, and everything we have.

Reflect

Do you only give when you feel confident? Or are you willing to offer your first out of faith and obedience to God?

Lord, I am willing to make an offering to you with all that I have. Amen.

Enthroned

You are holy, enthroned on the praises of Israel.

PSALM 22:3 ESV

Our verse today declares that God inhabits the praises of his people. This means that as we worship God, he draws near. We are inviting God into the room and into our circumstances, and his presence shifts the atmosphere. We can worship in song, words, action, and devotion.

We are in a spiritual battle, and worship is our weapon. Worship isn't just singing a song. It is obeying and believing God's authority over our lives. If the devil can't get Jesus to worship him, then he will try to come after us, who are made in the image of God, to worship him. Jesus is the only one worthy of our praise.

Reflect

Spend time worshiping God today. Worship him for who he is. Worship him for what he has done in your life. Worship him for his goodness. He deserves your praise.

*Lord, you are holy. Oh, my soul declares your goodness.
I praise your mighty name. Amen.*

What Is Good?

He has shown you, O mortal, what is good. And what does the LORD require of you? To act justly and to love mercy and to walk humbly with your God.

MICAH 6:8 NIV

We can't do anything to earn God's love. Our life is a response to the love we have received from God. We do not have to earn it. I have been married for over fifteen years, and I love my husband. I respect and admire him. I am kind to him not to earn his love but in response to my love for him. The same is true with our relationship with God.

As Jesus enters our life, we transform continually. We never stop growing and becoming more and more like Jesus. We love mercy, walk humbly with God, and act justly. People notice we are different—because we are.

Reflect

Are you humbly walking with God? Do you act justly? Spend time in prayer today thinking about these attributes.

I walk humbly with you, Father. Thank you for continually transforming my mind to yours. I praise you. Amen.

Anointed

As soon as Jesus was baptized, he went up out of the water.
At that moment heaven was opened, and he saw the Spirit of
God descending like a dove and alighting on him.

MATTHEW 3:16 NIV

We were created to be in the presence of God. Every day. In
biblical times, oil would be poured over the heads of kings,
priests, and prophets. The ritual of pouring aromatic oil over
a person's head is called *anointing*. We now have a spiritual
anointing as a result of being filled with the Holy Spirit. We
overflow and are baptized by the same Spirit of God that
descended on Jesus.

As we step into the reality of God's presence, our
lives change. Jesus, our King, anoints us. We see our days
through the lens of Jesus and eternity. This focus shifts our
perspective.

Reflect

Spend time today hosting the presence of God.
Go out and be mindful, yielding to God's Holy Spirit.

*Jesus, I want to live my life fully yielding to your Holy Spirit.
I am forever changed because of the anointing of your
presence, Lord. Amen.*

Give Thanks

Give thanks to the LORD, for he is good;
for his steadfast love endures forever!

1 CHRONICLES 16:34 ESV

Praise is the response of a grateful heart, and we have so much to be thankful for. God's character and presence are blessings, and his community is filled with brothers and sisters in Jesus to walk alongside us. From gorgeous sunsets to the star-filled night sky, beauty surrounds us.

It's hard to be bitter when we are thankful. And when we cultivate a thankful spirit, we take ourselves out of the center of our thoughts and create a thankful heart focused on the goodness of God. Let's forget about worshiping our problems. Instead, let's worship God, for his love lasts for eternity.

Reflect

Work on fostering a faithful heart, and when you start to become anxious or list stressors in your mind, choose to worship. Worship the Creator of the world.

Lord, your love endures forever.
I give you thanks today. Amen.

The Lord's Servant

"I am the Lord's servant," Mary answered.
"May your word to me be fulfilled." Then the angel left her.

LUKE 1:38 NIV

We can learn so much from Mary. She was obedient and faithful. She didn't understand God or have all the answers, but she identified herself as the Lord's servant. She knew God was faithful, so she placed her trust and her life in God's hands. He chose Mary to mother his beloved Son. I believe he chose her because he knew her heart. Because God knew that she trusted him, he was able to trust her. Can God trust you?

We often don't understand God. We don't have all the answers, and we can feel anxious and overwhelmed. We need to constantly remind ourselves that we are the Lord's servant. God is faithful, and he will fulfill his plans.

Reflect

Identify a desire that God has given you. If you don't feel you have one, ask God to provide one and make yourself available to listen and receive it from him.

Lord, I am your servant. May your word be fulfilled. Amen.

Fight the Good Fight

Fight the good fight of the faith. Take hold of the eternal life to which you were called and about which you made the good confession in the presence of many witnesses.

1 TIMOTHY 6:12 ESV

Paul is writing to his beloved son in the faith, Timothy, in our verse today. He is encouraging Timothy to do two things. First, Timothy is to "fight the good fight of the faith." Make no mistake, we are in a spiritual war while we are on earth.

Paul's second encouragement is to "take hold of the eternal life to which you were called." We must take hold of all God is offering us. We have the choice to believe and live a life of freedom or to live a life in bondage.

Reflect

What does "fight the good fight" mean in your life today?

Lord, I confess with my lips that I believe you are God.
I believe in my heart that you are Lord.
Help me to fight the good fight today. Amen.

One Thing

The Lord answered her, "Martha, Martha, you are anxious
and troubled about many things, but one thing is necessary.
Mary has chosen the good portion, which will not be
taken away from her."

LUKE 10:41–42 ESV

"You are anxious and troubled about many things," Jesus
said to Martha. Would Jesus say that to you too? Are you in
turmoil inside? Or are you focused on the one thing that is
necessary: Jesus.

As we shift our focus away from God and onto this
world, our hearts grow heavy. We become weighed down
by the worries of our day, and we can feel overwhelmed. We
must train ourselves to focus on Jesus. We must fan the flame
of our faith and fuel the fire of our relationship with God.

Reflect

Identify the things in your life that distract you from the
"one thing [that] is necessary." Be mindful today of focusing
on the one thing and let everything else fall
to the side of your focus.

*Lord, you are my one thing. I bow down to you and make
space for your presence today. You are with me,
and I worship you. Amen.*

Repentance

Do you presume on the riches of his kindness and forbearance and patience, not knowing that God's kindness is meant to lead you to repentance?

ROMANS 2:4 ESV

Paul writes about God's judgment in this chapter of Romans. God judges us while simultaneously pouring his grace over us. He doesn't give us what we deserve; he offers us forgiveness.

However, as we read today, his kindness should lead us into repentance. Because we see God is good and rich in mercy, we change our path and walk toward him. We repent. God desires our honest praise, love, and devotion. He isn't an angry Father ready to spank us when we mess up. We serve a loving God. He is patient and true. And as we receive his kindness, our hearts and lives transform.

Reflect

How has God been kind toward you lately?
Spend some time today thanking Jesus for his kindness.

Jesus, I am running toward you. I desire you. Thank you for your kindness and gentleness toward me. Amen.

Firstfruits

Honor the LORD with your wealth
and with the firstfruits of all your produce.

PROVERBS 3:9 ESV

Firstfruits means exactly what it sounds like: the best. The top. We don't wait to see how much time is left at the end of our day to pray. No, we schedule our quiet time with Jesus and make it happen. We tithe to our church and not out of what's left in our bank account at the end of the month, but out of the gate, we give.

Genesis 4 tells the story of Cain and Abel. Cain didn't give God his firstfruits, so his sacrifice didn't make God happy. We show God we value him above all else through our sacrifices. We worship God by sacrificing our time, our resources, and our money and by offering up our prayers to him.

Reflect

Give God the "firstfruits of your produce" today.

Jesus, I offer you my firstfruits to honor you. Amen.

Real People, Real Issues

*This is the genealogy of Jesus the Messiah the son of David,
the son of Abraham: Abraham was the father of Isaac,
Isaac the father of Jacob, Jacob the father of Judah
and his brothers.*

MATTHEW 1:1–2 NIV

Many of the men and women listed in the first chapter of
Matthew are heroes of our faith. Our verses from Matthew
today list the names of Jesus' ancestors. Abraham walked
and talked to God in an intimate way, for example, and King
David is described as a man after God's own heart. However,
as we dig deeper, we realize that this list of names is full of
real people, just like us, with real issues.

I don't know about you, but I find it comforting to know
that Jesus understands and experienced firsthand a family
full of dysfunction. Everyone, even the heroes in our lives,
will inevitably let us down. People are people, flawed and full
of sin. That's why we look to Jesus to be the hero of our life.

Reflect

Think about any unresolved issues you have within
your family line. Pray about them and leave them
at the feet of Jesus today.

*Lord, thank you for sending your Son and for understanding
my issues and dysfunctions. Amen.*

Our Hearts

A person may think their own ways are right,
but the LORD weighs the heart.

PROVERBS 21:2 NIV

We read lots of verses in the Bible about our hearts. We know our hearts can be hardened (Mark 6:52). We are encouraged to guard our hearts above all else (Proverbs 4:23), and God can create in us a pure heart (Psalm 51:10). Our verse today tells us two important points to add to our list about our hearts.

First, we see that our heart can deceive us. In our heart, we can feel fully justified, but our heart can be foolish and lead us astray. This is why knowing God's Word, having believers in our life, and praying will help guide us. Second, we see that God weighs our heart. He knows our innermost being and our intentions. Righteousness pleases him while sin disappoints.

Reflect

Examine your heart honestly before God today. Talk to him about your desires and where your heart is leading you. Let the Lord reveal things to you as he weighs your heart.

Create in me a pure heart, God. I want to pursue only you and your will for my life. Amen.

Life and Peace

Those who live according to the flesh have their minds set on what the flesh desires; but those who live in accordance with the Spirit have their minds set on what the Spirit desires. The mind governed by the flesh is death, but the mind governed by the Spirit is life and peace.

ROMANS 8:5–6 NIV

I desire to live in accordance with the Spirit. What does that mean? Paul explains that it's setting our minds on what the Spirit desires. The verse ends with the beautiful thought that our minds, when governed by the Holy Spirit, will lead us into life and peace.

I want to love life. I want to feel alive. I picture a child at the beach, running in total peace and freedom. Playing in the sea without a single care in the world. Peaceful. Joyful. This is what God offers us today, sweet sister. Take it. It's yours.

Reflect

Intentionally allow God to govern your mind today.

Lord, I desire to live according to your Spirit. Pour your presence over me and shift the atmosphere. Amen.

December

Living Sacrifice

I urge you, brothers and sisters, in view of God's mercy, to offer your bodies as a living sacrifice, holy and pleasing to God—this is your true and proper worship.

ROMANS 12:1 NIV

We are called to be a living sacrifice to God. We can do so by presenting our lives to God as an act of worship. Would the Lord describe your life as holy and pleasing?

We know that we aren't perfect and that Jesus was the ultimate sacrifice for the sins of the world. Yes, we no longer have to atone for our shortcomings. However, we are held accountable for our faith. Our lives are the response that God demands for all he has done for us.

Reflect

Offer yourself as a living sacrifice to God today.

Lord, I am yours. I desire to be holy and pleasing.
I am so excited for the adventure you have prepared for me.
Open my eyes to see your work all around me.
Let me be a light to bring you glory. Amen.

Testimony

They have defeated him by the blood of the Lamb
and by their testimony.

REVELATION 12:11 NLT

Jesus triumphs over evil. We have eternal life because he
conquered death on the cross. Our verse today enlists us
in the battle of darkness over light. To defeat darkness, the
blood of the Lamb and the words of our testimony are used.
Our story has power. Words can spark a revolution!

The Bible is full of stories of people who encounter God
and who have triumphed because of him. When God shows
up for you, he wants you to share that story with others.
Hearing how God has shown up in our lives fans the flames
of our faith. Your story matters in God's kingdom. Share it!

Reflect

Share your faith testimony with someone today.

Jesus, give me the courage to be bold and share my faith.
Provide opportunities for me to speak into those around me.
Thank you for being so present in my life, Lord. Give me the
words to communicate that to others. Amen.

Messiah

An angel of the Lord appeared to them, and the glory of the
Lord shone around them, and they were terrified. But the
angel said to them, "Do not be afraid. I bring you good news
that will cause great joy for all the people. Today in the town
of David a Savior has been born to you;
he is the Messiah, the Lord."

LUKE 2:9–11 NIV

In Judaism, the Messiah was the expected king of the
Davidic line who would deliver Israel from foreign bondage
and restore the glories of its golden age. The Anointed One.
The King of kings.

The Jews' expectation of this promise looked a certain
way: Jesus would be strong and political. But the King of
kings, the Messiah, operates in the spiritual realm, setting us
free and delivering us from bondage. He calls us to a life of
freedom. We have hope because we have the Messiah.

Reflect

During the busy holiday season, intentionally slow down.
Make room for God to reveal himself to you
in unexpected moments.

*Lord, you are my good news. You are my hope,
my Savior, my Messiah. Amen.*

Shaped by God

"Your hands shaped me and made me."

JOB 10:8 NIV

God has shaped you. Not only has he shaped you, but our Creator has also prepared you in advance to give him glory. We are the hands and feet of Jesus on this side of heaven. God made you, every unique, beautiful part of you, and you matter to him. Nothing about you is an accident.

Our God is a creative God. Look at the changing colors of the sky or the details of a flower. He created us with such imagination and love. God values imagination. He has given us an anointing.

Reflect

Spend time today thanking God for the way he has made you. Be specific about how he has shaped you and thank him for the way you are.

Lord, thank you for being the Creator. You have made me, and I am so grateful for who I am. Amen.

Sons of Thunder

James son of Zebedee and his brother John (to them he gave
the name Boanerges, which means "sons of thunder").

MARK 3:17 NIV

Jesus has a purpose for everything he does. He gave James
and John the nickname "sons of thunder." I desire to have
such a close relationship with Jesus that he has a nickname
like that for me! Nevertheless, as we dig into Scripture, we
see references to James and John being a bit "thunderous."
For example, in Luke 9, we read about the disciples and Jesus
not finding accommodations for the night while they are
traveling. In verse 54 (niv), James and John ask, "Lord, do
you want us to call fire down from heaven to destroy them?"
Our beloved sons of thunder were coming in hot!

Jesus loves every quality that we have, even the ones that
we have come to believe are negative traits. I would describe
myself as a bit of a hothead like James and John. But as I
learn to submit to Jesus' will in my life, those edges continue
to soften.

Reflect

What nickname would Jesus give you?

Thank you for knowing me intimately, Lord.
You love me, and I am yours. Amen.

Fasting

"When you fast, do not look somber as the hypocrites do,
for they disfigure their faces to show others they are fasting.
Truly I tell you, they have received their reward in full."

MATTHEW 6:16 NIV

The first word of this verse gives us pause. Jesus doesn't say "*If
you fast*"; he declares "*When you fast.*" We are expected to fast,
and it isn't limited to food. You can also fast from Instagram,
shopping, television, sugar, alcohol, or something else.

What you hunger for the most is what you value the
most. Fasting tells your flesh nature to yield. It's giving up
something you love for something you love even more. Pay
attention to what you think about and offer that to God
during your fast. Our appetites can be so powerful, but our
heart's desire is to have an appetite for God.

Reflect

Fast at some point this week. Ask God what he wants you to
take a break from and use the extra time to draw near
and focus on him.

*Lord, I desire you. I desire your presence and your power in
my life. Guide me in my fast and bless this time, Lord. Amen.*

Fresh Manna

The Lord said to Moses, "Look, I'm going to rain down food
from heaven for you. Each day the people can go out and
pick up as much food as they need for that day. I will test
them in this to see whether or not they will
follow my instructions."

EXODUS 16:4 NLT

The Lord provided Moses and the Israelites enough for their
day. Generations later, Jesus taught us to pray the Lord's
Prayer. Part of this prayer was to ask God for daily provision,
"Give us today our daily bread" (Matthew 6:11 NIV).

God gives us fresh manna every day. He doesn't give us
more than we can handle. He gives us just enough. We must
still have faith for provision for tomorrow. We cannot rely on
the past, whether it's good or bad. God has something new
for us today and every day, and it is enough.

Reflect

Look for the fresh, new thing that God has prepared
for you today. Keep your eyes open for his goodness.

*Lord, thank you for your provision in my life. I trust you with
my future, and that starts today. Amen.*

Stay with God

I'm sure now I'll see God's goodness in the exuberant earth.
Stay with GOD! Take heart. Don't quit. I'll say it again:
Stay with GOD.

PSALM 27:13–14 MSG

The holidays can feel so hectic, stressful, and overwhelming with all of the busyness and expectations that come with them. Did we buy enough gifts? Did we buy too many gifts? Did we do all of the magical holiday activities to make the season a special and memorable one?

When we get caught up in the chaos, we can remember and rest in today's promise. We will see the goodness of God in this world. In the smiles of our loved ones. In the glistening of snowflakes. In the kindness of one stranger to another. Let's take heart and stay with God, the anchor of our souls.

Reflect

Find God's goodness in someone or something today.

Lord, no storm is too great, for you offer glorious hope.
Thank you for anchoring my soul. I stay with you. Amen.

Pouring of His Spirit

"I will pour out my Spirit on all people. Your sons and daughters will prophesy, your old men will dream dreams, your young men will see visions."

JOEL 2:28 NIV

God pours his Spirit on us. He speaks to us through his Word and through our worship, prayer, and dreams. He is holy and just. He is righteous and pure.

We tend to focus on all the problems in our life, the chaos and unrest in the world, or other concerns outside of our control. But when we pause to appreciate the goodness of God, we feel our souls lift, and we shine the light of Jesus on everyone we meet. Receive God's Spirit and focus on his living water.

Reflect

Walk through your day in the reality that God's Spirit has been poured out on you.

Jesus, I desire to hold the anointing you have on my life. I know I am called, and my heart's desire is to glorify you in all I do. Amen.

God's Family

You will know how people must conduct themselves in
the household of God. This is the church of the living God,
which is the pillar and foundation of the truth.

1 TIMOTHY 3:15 NLT

From the moment God created humans, he knew "it is not
good for the man to be alone" (Genesis 2:18 NIV). God's
family is his church, and as believers, we belong to his family.
It's important for us to plug ourselves into his community.

I became a Christian as a freshman in high school and
experienced this inclusion firsthand. My church community
today has the same Spirit and sense of family that I felt over
twenty years ago. We are united in Jesus. His Spirit is the
same because it is unchanging and eternal. When you are in
a room of believers, you are home.

Reflect

Do something for your local church today. Text
encouragement to your pastor, join a small group, or invite
someone to join you on Sunday. If you aren't part of a local,
faith-filled community, what are you waiting for?

Lord, I pray for your family, your church.
I pray for leaders to rise and for a movement of faith
that will transform our world. Amen.

Abundant Faith

He did not do many miracles there
because of their lack of faith.

MATTHEW 13:58 NIV

I watched the movie *Elf* with my boys, and at the end of the movie, Santa's sleigh cannot fly because people have stopped believing in him. Obviously, Jesus isn't Santa, so he doesn't have this problem. Jesus is God and all powerful. He has the ability to call on thousands of angels, and they would appear. Yet he chooses not to for our sake. It feels weird, at least to me, to think that Jesus' display of power is connected with our faith.

We have free will and can choose to believe in miracles, or we can place our life and faith in what we can see with our earthly eyes. The latter doesn't require any faith. But we want our lives to operate in the supernatural. We were created to worship a big and mighty God. Let's have some bold faith! Let's pray some bold prayers! Let's witness miracles in our life because of our abundant faith.

Reflect

Pray bold prayers today to draw closer to Christ
and usher in his miracles.

Help with my unbelief, Lord.
I want to see your miracles all around me. Amen.

What We Do

You can tell what they are by what they do.

MATTHEW 7:16 CEV

As believers, we are called to a higher standard, so our integrity matters a great deal. We are called to be trustworthy, faithful, pure, and forgiving. We are called to love. We don't have a checklist of attributes that we have to attain to be considered mature in our faith. We simply live our faith out loud. As we draw near to Jesus, he draws near to us. We start to act and sound like Jesus because of the time we spend with him.

If we confess we believe, then our lives will reflect that conviction. I love my children, and I demonstrate that love by the energy I pour into them and the sacrifices that I make for them. The time that I put into being a good, loving mom expresses to them how much I love them. The same is true with our relationship with God.

Reflect

Take an unbiased inventory of your actions from this past week. What can you learn about your values from how you spent your days?

Jesus, I worship you in Spirit and in truth. You are my King, and I give you full access to my life. Amen.

Seal of Ownership

It is God who makes both us and you stand firm in Christ.
He anointed us, set his seal of ownership on us,
and put his Spirit in our hearts as a deposit,
guaranteeing what is to come.

2 CORINTHIANS 1:21–22 NIV

God has done everything for us to have great faith and live a life of boldness. He sent his Son to model how to live for us. Jesus died and conquered death so that we would be assured that the sting of death was defeated.

He tells us today through our verse that he anoints us. We are not just anointed, but we also have a seal of ownership on us in the spiritual realm. He gives us his Holy Spirit in our hearts not only to remind us but also as a guarantee to us of what is to come. There is so much power in the Lord.

Reflect

Think about your anointing. You are set apart
to serve God in your own unique way.

*Lord, I stand firm in my faith in you. Thank you for the seal
you have placed over me and the anointing on my life. Amen.*

Halted Plans

Because Joseph her husband was faithful to the law, and yet
did not want to expose her to public disgrace,
he had in mind to divorce her quietly.

MATTHEW 1:19 NIV

I love that God's Word tells stories about real people who
have doubts, make mistakes, and face fears just like I do.
Joseph was engaged to be married. He was a good, young,
Jewish man. But when he found out that his future wife was
pregnant, all of his plans came to a halt.

God tends to do that a lot with his people. He halts our
plans for his will. We can choose to trust him through the
pain or uncertainty, or we can try to control the people and
situations around us. It is so wonderfully freeing to just let
go. To let go and let God. No matter what happens to our
plans, we find rest, joy, and peace in God's presence. No one
can take that away from us.

Reflect

What plan are you holding on tightly to?
Hand that over to God today.

I trust your plan for me, Jesus. Amen.

Eternal Life

This is eternal life: that they know you, the only true God,
and Jesus Christ, whom you have sent.

JOHN 17:3 NIV

Our faith is not based on what we know about Jesus but
that we know Jesus. The more we know and encounter the
living God, the more eternity and the things of heaven start
to crack open in our lives. What a gift and a blessing of total
grace that we can encounter and know God!

The only true God sent Jesus Christ to earth so that we
could have eternal life. The Bible tells us that eternity is set in
our hearts. Our souls are made for eternity, and we yearn for
the things of heaven because that is what we are created for.

Reflect

Set your mind today on the things of eternity.
Think about things that are pure, true, lovely, and positive.
Train your mind today in your thoughts.

Lord, you are the only true God. You are holy, righteous,
faithful, and pure. I love you with all that I am.
I want to know you more deeply. I make myself
available to you, Lord. Amen.

God's Glory

According to the riches of his glory he may grant you to be strengthened with power through his Spirit in your inner being, so that Christ may dwell in your hearts through faith.

EPHESIANS 3:16–17 ESV

There are riches in God's glory. What does that really, tangibly mean? I believe God is telling us that as we align with God's will for our lives, we will see God's glory. I have seen and experienced this in my own life. As I have taken steps in faith, in things that I know God is calling me to step into, the supernatural happens. And God's glory is the explanation behind it.

We are called to be rooted and grounded in love. This means that we have faith to allow God to do what he is capable of in our lives.

Reflect

There is so much promise and power in our Scripture verse today. Take a moment to read it again, perhaps out loud this time. Take your time and truly ponder the promises.

Lord, you are capable of everything. Nothing is impossible with you. I give you glory and honor with my whole life. Amen.

Children of God

Do all things without grumbling or disputing, that you may be blameless and innocent, children of God without blemish in the midst of a crooked and twisted generation, among whom you shine as lights in the world, holding fast to the word of life, so that in the day of Christ I may be proud that I did not run in vain or labor in vain.

PHILIPPIANS 2:14–16 ESV

Shine as lights in this world! How do we do this? By holding fast to the Word. Many of us want to shine and be used by God and have a big, bold faith. And yet we aren't in a Bible study or communing with our church. Or we aren't spending time in the Word. Or we rely on secondhand encounters with Jesus to strengthen our faith.

Yes, having Scripture explained to you by your pastor on Sunday is good, but God wants one-on-one time with you as well. He has things to reveal to you in ways that only he can. God's love language is quality time. Let's be a generation that puts time and effort into our faith.

Reflect

Make your faith your priority today.

Jesus, I am set apart for your glory. Amen.

In Jesus

For the Son of God, Jesus Christ, who was preached among you by us—by me and Silas and Timothy—was not "Yes" and "No," but in him it has always been "Yes." For no matter how many promises God has made, they are "Yes" in Christ. And so through him the "Amen" is spoken by us to the glory of God.

2 CORINTHIANS 1:19–20 NIV

Do you know the promises God gives us? His promises to us are yes in Jesus. He tells us he will never leave us or forsake us (see Hebrews 13:5). He declares that he will make all things work for the good of those who love him (see Romans 8:28). He knows us, loves us, formed us, and is with us (see Psalm 139). His ways are above all ways, and he is good, faithful, holy, and true.

No matter how many times we may have felt let down, deserted, or uncertain, God's promises are true. In Jesus, we have a yes for all eternity.

Reflect

Try to be a yes person today.

Jesus, thank you for all your promises to me.
I know they are for the glory of God.
I say yes, Lord, yes. Amen.

Those Who Dream

When the LORD restored the fortunes of Zion,
we were like those who dream.

PSALM 126:1 ESV

We chase after dreams that don't require or involve our faith, and then we wonder why we are left feeling unsatisfied and unfulfilled. We are called to dream a dream and lead a life that requires the movement of God. God can do more than we can imagine, so dream big, sweet sister.

Nothing honors God more than our faith. We trust God with our life, expecting and taking risks we can only accomplish through him. I have heard it said that many people overestimate what they can do short term and underestimate what they can do long term. Imagine if we added God to that equation. I can personally testify that my life is richer than I ever could have imagined, and I believe it's because I continuously make space for God to do the miraculous.

Reflect

Be a dreamer today. Spend time dreaming with God.
Talk to him about your dreams.

*Jesus, I place the desires of my heart at your feet.
Use me, Father. Amen.*

Be Watchful

Be always on the watch, and pray that you may be able to escape all that is about to happen, and that you may be able to stand before the Son of Man.

LUKE 21:36 NIV

Many verses connect watchfulness with prayer. In other words, the more we pray, the more we notice what God is up to all around us. Prayer gives us wings and opens our spiritual eyes. The Aramaic word for "prayer" means to "set a trap."[14] Prayer is the way we take our thoughts captive.

I never considered myself a prayer warrior early in my faith journey. I have always loved reading God's Word, but I would find quiet times sometimes dry, feeling forced or obligated to do it. I had to learn to pray. Now I value prayer on a deeper level and have seen the movement of God in my heart through my prayers. I can tell when my spirit is more anxious or on edge, and it's always when I haven't spent time with Jesus.

Reflect

Pray today and then be watchful.

Jesus, I desire your presence. You are my heart's desire. Amen.

---

14 Rocco A. Errico, "The Ancient Aramaic Prayer of Jesus—'The Lord's Prayer,'" Holy Trinity Ukrainian Catholic Church (website).

Honor

Jesus said to them, "A prophet is not without honor,
except in his hometown and among his relatives and
in his own household."

MARK 6:4 ESV

Our focus today is on the word *honor*. The Greek word for
"honor" is *timé*. The literal definition of *timé* is "a value;
esteem (especially of the highest degree)."[15] Do you value
God? How do you honor him? Do you demonstrate your
reverence for him in your life by what you do, what you
think about, and what you spend your money, talent, and
resources on? All of these things are reflective of your heart.

We are called to become more and more like Jesus every
day. This includes honoring the things Jesus honors. Jesus
values everyone. He honors love, peace, life, and truth. He
values prayer, relationships, and fasting. As we draw closer to
Jesus, our hearts transform into the things of eternity.

Reflect

Be mindful to value God and all that he values.

*Lord, I desire my heart to conform more and more
to be like yours. I want to value what you value,
honor what you honor. Amen.*

---

15   Strong, *Strong's Expanded Exhaustive Concordance of the
Bible*, #5099.

A Cheerful Heart

A cheerful heart is good medicine,
but a broken spirit saps a person's strength.

PROVERBS 17:22 NLT

We all have broken spirits sometimes. And it's true that whatever has us feeling down, disappointed, or sad can also make us feel tired and weak. The truth is that none of us gets joy from feeling upset or lingering in negativity.

When we need to find joy, all we have to do is remember the many promises of God. Look toward heaven and appreciate everything that we have to look forward to. In heaven, we receive new bodies free of aches, pains, and diseases. We will never feel hurt, lonely, or scared. We will be united and forever in the presence of the Lord, our maker, who sent his Son so that we could receive his glorious promises.

Reflect

Let your faith and the promises of God
make your heart cheerful today.

*When I am down, I find comfort and joy in you, Lord.
Thank you for your great promises. I know that you will
fulfill them, and that makes my heart cheerful.*

A Good Word

Anxiety in a man's heart weighs him down,
but a good word makes him glad.

PROVERBS 12:25 ESV

I am not making light of real and complex issues, but I do believe anxiety is one of our biggest threats on the battlefield of day-to-day life. Addictions, eating disorders, and insomnia are often wrapped around troubling anxieties. And our anxious thoughts that turn into anxious words sometimes get us into trouble too.

Are you or someone you know in search of a good word? The Bible is full of promises to "make [us] glad," as today's verse from Proverbs shares. If we want to live a life of joy, then we have to come with truth, and not our own truth about our life, our thoughts, and our chains, but God's truth. We can't allow our worry to sit inside of us and cause anxiety. God can handle our dysfunction, and he doesn't fear our darkness. We can bring our doubts and pains and lay them before our Savior.

Reflect

What is stressing you out today? Visualize yourself bringing your stress to Jesus and laying it at his feet.

Lord, I desire a good word today. Thank you for your promises of hope and love. I cling to you, Jesus. Amen.

Overjoyed

When they saw the star, they were overjoyed.

MATTHEW 2:10 NIV

Imagine the joy and wonder the magi felt as they followed the star through the night. What a step of faith they put into practice! Tradition depicts the magi next to a manger with a baby, but history actually suggests that they wandered in the desert for around two years before the star led them to Jesus.

I try to imagine all the emotions they must have felt over the span of time that they followed the star. Wonder and joy. Faith and anticipation. The conversations they must have had on the road as they were led to Jesus, the King of kings. The same can be true for us today. God is all around us, leading us on a great adventure if we open our eyes to see his fingerprints all over our lives.

Reflect

Don't lose your joy and wonder this Christmas.
Focus on his presence instead of presents.

Lord, I pray I don't miss out on your wonder all around me. You are a God of joy, and my heart loves your presence. Amen.

With Us

"The virgin will conceive and give birth to a son, and they will call him Immanuel" (which means "God with us").

MATTHEW 1:23 NIV

Today we celebrate Jesus' birth! Perhaps the truth and power of Jesus has grown so familiar that it has lost its meaning or significance in your heart. God, the all-powerful, all-knowing, infinite, and eternal being laid aside his glory and made himself a man, born as a baby. For you. What a moving, powerful act of love.

God is always with us. He is protecting us, guiding us, and ruling us. Perhaps we have felt unprotected by God at times. Maybe we have felt let down by Jesus at one time or another. Remember that God's ways are above ours. He will use everything we endure for good, even if it is intended for harm. The God we serve is powerful, loving, faithful, and true.

Reflect

Remember that God is with you today and every day. In every situation you face, he is beside you and protecting you.

Jesus, I pray I will remember the true meaning of today. Help me not to feel too busy or overwhelmed to celebrate and focus on you. Amen.

Helping Those in Need

"Through it all, you've never deserted your fellow Israelites and were always there to help them."

JOSHUA 22:3 TPT

The beauty of this verse is that it celebrates community and helping one another out. The truth is that we all need each other. We all experience times of trouble, and it's incredibly helpful and encouraging to have others rally around us in support.

Helpers are heroes. I'm reminded of how we celebrated frontline workers during the COVID-19 pandemic. Think of all the signs and posts we saw lifting them up in thanks and support. Imagine the trouble we would have been in had it not been for their sacrifice, dedication, and bravery. May we continue to lift up others every day, living as servants of Jesus.

Reflect

What can you do today to help someone else? Cook a meal, say a kind word, open a door. It doesn't matter how big or small the act, but show up for someone else today.

Lord, I want to be a helper. Open my eyes to someone in need today so that I might shine your mercy, grace, and goodness to her. Amen.

Salvation

"Salvation belongs to our God,
who sits on the throne, and to the Lamb."
REVELATION 7:10 NIV

How amazing is it that salvation belongs to God? I always pictured my salvation, my testimony, and my faith as my own, but knowing that it belongs to God gives it a certain worth, weight, and even adds his holiness to it. It adds more joy to my heart knowing that my faith is a gift from God.

If you are struggling with chains of anxiety, depression, fear, anger, or anything else, then cry out to Jesus. We were not created to live in captivity. It is through God's grace and our faith in Jesus Christ that we are saved. Salvation belongs to the Lord, who sits on the throne, and he offers salvation to us freely with open arms. We are set free for eternity, and that freedom starts now.

Reflect

Imagine God on the heavenly throne. Thank him for your salvation while you picture this image.

Lord, I thank you for the gift of salvation. Thank you for your grace, your love, and your Son, Jesus Christ. Amen.

Unshakable Joy

After you have suffered a little while, the God of all grace,
who has called you to his eternal glory in Christ, will himself
restore, confirm, strengthen, and establish you.

1 PETER 5:10 ESV

My life has been full of hardship, pain, disease, and darkness,
but I can stand firm and claim that my life has been good.
I have seen and experienced the joy of love, friendship,
community, and healing, even in the midst of heartbreak and
sorrow. Perhaps you, too, have experienced the joy of being
restored by the Lord.

The charge at the end of this verse is that God himself
will "restore, confirm, strengthen, and establish" us, and each
of those words carries such hope and strength. We must
remember that moments don't define us; they develop us. As
we seek God in every situation, we not only find him, but we
also find joy. That kind of joy cannot be shaken.

Reflect

Allow God to restore you today. That will look different for
each of us. Maybe it's a prayer of release, a phone call of
forgiveness, or something entirely different.
Invite restoration into your life.

*Lord, you have called me to eternal glory. You promise to
restore, strengthen, and establish me. I claim these promises
over my life today in your name, Jesus. Amen.*

A Hard Worker

She goes to inspect a field and buys it; with her earnings she plants a vineyard. She is energetic and strong, a hard worker.

PROVERBS 31:16–17 NLT

If you're not familiar with Proverbs 31, this chapter describes the heart of a godly, virtuous woman. It offers insight into who she is and what she does, and many women look to the descriptions for guidance and aspirational goals on how to conduct themselves and develop their own character.

What I love about today's verse in particular is that it discusses a godly woman's work ethic. Notice how she "inspects" a field before buying it. Other translations use the word "considers" instead. Regardless, she's careful and thoughtful about her decisions. She doesn't buy impulsively; she uses her wisdom. And she buys the field with her own earnings no less. Then she plants a vineyard, working energetically and with strength. Let's be hard workers like the Proverbs 31 woman.

Reflect

Read all of Proverbs 31 today and let it inspire you to keep growing and developing your character.

Lord, I am a woman after your heart. I seek you in all that I do and aspire to be a godly, virtuous woman. Amen.

Open Door

> "I have placed before you an open door that no one can shut.
> I know that you have little strength, yet you have kept my
> word and have not denied my name."
>
> REVELATION 3:8 NIV

When God opens a door for us, no one can stop us from going through it. Not even ourselves. We may not know what's on the other side, and the shadow of uncertainty might make it appear dark or threatening. We may not feel ready to cross through it or simply too scared to take the first step. That's okay.

New beginnings can be scary, but they're part of our journey. Even if we feel too weak, as though we're running out of strength, God will carry us through and give us the strength that we need. The journey will come with bumps along the way, but God is always beside us, guiding us. He wants good things for us: freedom, joy, peace, victory, and love. Trust him. Grab hold of his hand and let him lead the way.

Reflect

Recall a time when God opened a door for you.
How did he see you through it?

*Even when I am fearful or unsure, I know that I can trust
the doors you open for me, Lord. Help me take the first step
toward the new beginning you have destined for me. Amen.*

Run Your Race

> "As for you, be strong and do not give up,
> for your work will be rewarded."
>
> 2 CHRONICLES 15:7 NIV

Our closing verse of the year encourages us to persevere.
It's often in times of struggle that we see where our true
hope lies. We will want to give up sometimes, especially
when life isn't going the way we expected. But when we feel
discouraged or lost, remember the words of Hebrews 12:1–2:
"Let us run with endurance the race that is set before us,
looking to Jesus" (ESV).

Patience is hard, and no one likes to wait, but God
values commitment, honor, and integrity. When he calls us
to do or experience something, he provides a way through
it. When we're facing the fires of life, he strips away our
comfort and control but stays beside us, gently guiding us.
It is never easy to walk through the flames, but the qualities
that emerge within us are more beautiful than gold.

Reflect

Run your race. Do not give up. Continue to seek the Lord
and boldly stand for Jesus, however that looks
for you in your life.

*Lord, I desire your will for my life. I will not give up,
and I will seek you in all the days of my life. Amen.*

Acknowledgments

I feel overwhelmed with the community that Jesus has blessed me with. My family has always been my biggest cheerleader, and my mom and dad encouraged seeking God and his spiritual truths.

Some of my favorite childhood memories are with my youth ministry leaders, specifically Bob, Kurt, Tim, and Casey. Thank you for showing me through example what it looks like to follow Jesus.

My husband, Doug, could not be more supportive. His belief in me is a constant comfort and source of inspiration. My three boys also walked through the writing process with me, and I won't be surprised if one of them becomes a bestselling author in their own right!

Thank you to my pastors at Oceans Church and my Bible study girls of SWAG and Tribe, who constantly prayed not only for me but also for the readers of this devotional. They all helped to make this book a reality. It truly takes a village, and I am so grateful for mine.

I wanted to take a moment to thank you. It has been a privilege to read and study God's Word with you. I have been praying for you, trying to picture each beautiful face on this journey with me. God is so good, and his Word is rich with power, grace, and love. I will continue to pray for you, sweet sister.

About the Author

Lydia McLaughlin has been a Christian for over twenty-five years and uses the platform God has given her to inspire women to make their faith a reality. She speaks at women's conferences and leads Instagram live Bible studies, some of which she herself has written. She is also an on-air personality, author, and magazine editor for luxury men's magazine *NOBLEMAN,* which she and her husband, Doug, own and publish.

Lydia grew up in the television industry in Newfoundland, Canada, and has always felt right at home in front of the camera. She joined the season eight cast of *The Real Housewives of Orange County* and was notably vocal about her spiritual beliefs. She took a break from the show to have her third son but returned for season twelve to utilize the show's platform to be a light. She is such a fan favorite that she and her mother partnered with Bravo TV in 2020 to launch their digital series *Glitter Town.* Viewers loved watching the mother-daughter duo spread love and joy wherever they went.

Most proud of her roles as wife and mother, Lydia has been married to Doug for more than fifteen years. They love to travel and experience new adventures together and have three boys: Stirling, Maverick, and Roman.

To stay connected with Lydia and join the online community, follow her @oclydia.

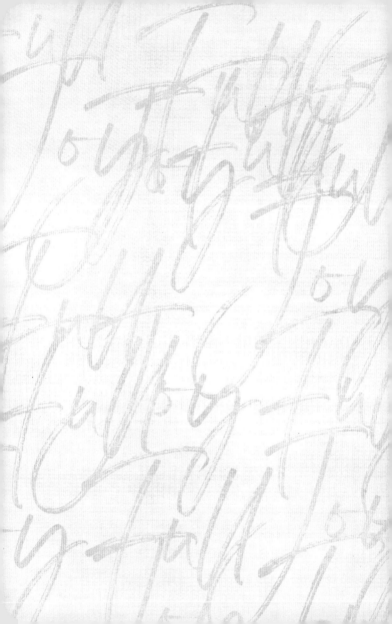